THE
QUILT
ENCYCLOPEDIA
ILLUSTRATED

BY CARTER HOUCK

FOREWORD BY ROBERT BISHOP AND ELIZABETH WARREN

THE
QUILT
ENCYCLOPEDIA
ILLUSTRATED

HARRY N. ABRAMS, INC., PUBLISHERS, NEW YORK
IN ASSOCIATION WITH THE MUSEUM OF AMERICAN FOLK ART

EDITOR: DARLENE GEIS
DESIGNER: ANA ROGERS

Library of Congress Cataloging-in-Publication Data

Houck, Carter.
    The quilt encyclopedia illustrated: designs, patterns, techniques,
    equipment, conservation and care, textiles, dyes, history, quilt
    organizations and publications, and more. / Carter Houck:
    foreword by Robert Bishop and Elizabeth Warren
        p. cm.
    ISBN 0-8109-3457-4
    1. Quilts — Dictionaries. I. Museum of American Folk Art.
    II. Title.
    NK9104.H68   1991
    746.9'7'03—dc20

PHOTO CREDITS

COLOR: Steven Attig, (p. 147), Peter Gledinning, (p. 20), Michael Keller, (pp. 79, 126 left),
Myron Miller, (pp. 1, 2, 10, 11 bottom, 13 top, 14 bottom, 19 bottom, 24, 25 right, 26 bottom,
27, 29, 31, 32, 35, 37 bottom right, 40, 41 left, 43, 44 left, 46 bottom right, 52 bottom, 55,
57, 58, 61, 62 top, 68, 75, 76 middle, 77, 79, 81 bottom, 82 right, 84, 86, 87, 90, 91 top, 92,
95, 96, 102 bottom, 106, 113 bottom, 114, 117, 120 bottom, 122, 123, 126 right, 130, 132,
134, 135, 136, 140 left, 143, 145, 148, 149, 150 bottom, 151, 153, 155, 156, 160 top, 161,
162, 163 right, 164, 167 right, 168, 170, 175, 176, 177, 178, 179, 180 top, 188, 189),
Mark Weinkle, (pp. 14, 30, 46 right, 53 top, 69 bottom)
BLACK AND WHITE: Come Quilt with Me (p. 22 right), Myron Miller (pp. 22 right, 23, 34,
37 right, 39 left, 48, 52 right, 53 left, 64 left, 65 left, 100, 109, 120 right, 121 left, 127,
131 above left, 146 right, 150 right, 152 right, 154 right, 158, 160 right, 167 left, 169 right,
172, 185), Norwood Looms, Freemont, Michigan, (p.76)

FIRST PAGE: The Soul of Medieval Italy is comprised of nine scenes of daily life, as
shown in drawings in a fifteenth-century Italian manuscript, *Tacuinum Sanitatis*.
The quilt was designed and made in 1987 by Suzanne Marshall. 71 x 79″

SECOND PAGE: Spider Web is a strip- or string-pieced pattern based on an octagon.
Zoorett Freeman of West Virginia uses newspaper to stabilize her blocks until
they are all sewn together

FOREWORD

When Jonathan Holstein and Gail van der Hoof curated the exhibition "Abstract Design in American Quilts" at the Whitney Museum in 1971, no one could have predicted the success of the show or the floodgate of enthusiasm it opened in the art world for so modest an everyday object as a bedcover. After all, a quilt was a simple utilitarian object created by a needlewoman who was not a trained artist. Many of the textiles were without histories, frequently separated by years and miles from the women and the communities that had created and used them. Furthermore, there were few collectors who considered quilts worthy of serious study and preservation.

The exhibition was a resounding triumph. It captured the imagination of art critics, art historians, textile enthusiasts, quiltmakers, and, finally, collectors. This trailblazing show was the unquestioned beginning of America's appreciation of the quilt as a work of art.

While we at the Museum of American Folk Art have long known that quilts are by far the most popular category of folk art — quilt exhibitions always generate the largest attendance, lectures about quilts frequently sell out, and quilt books are the perennial best-sellers in our shops — the appeal of quilts to a wide general audience was made abundantly clear to us by the success of the biennial Great American Quilt Festival on Pier 92 in New York. The exhibitions on the pier, the many lectures and symposia, and the sold-out workshops attest to the phenomenal enthusiasm for quilts abroad in the land.

What was also made clear was the almost unquenchable desire of this vast audience for any and all information about quilts. It is a mixed audience, composed of quilt collectors, art historians, and — perhaps the greatest number of all — quiltmakers. Many of these people frequently ask members of the Museum staff to recommend one book that they can use as a standard reference for quilts of all kinds. It has been impossible for us to do this. While there are many good books on quilts available, they are almost all highly specialized, or else they are price guides and picture books without much text. One of the earliest and best general reference works on quilts, *Quilts in America* by Myron and Patsy Orlofsky, has been out of print for a number of years, and some of its information would now be out of date.

Clearly this is the time for a general quilt encyclopedia that sums up the current state of knowledge and the basic information about the subject. Carter Houck, the author of *The Quilt Encyclopedia Illustrated*, is a writer and lecturer who has played a central role in increasing appreciation for the quilt today. As editor for many years of *Lady's Circle Patchwork Quilts* she brought to a national constituency an awareness of antique quilts as well as of the works of art being created by the contemporary needlewoman. Her critical opinions have shaped the taste of present-day quiltmakers, for she judges quilt contests often, and continues to write on the subject so dear to her.

The romance of the patchwork quilt is no longer just an American phenomenon. Important collections have been formed in England, France, Germany, Italy, Japan, Denmark, Holland, and Switzerland. The Japanese are perhaps the most avid enthusiasts. They collect American quilts, they collect antique Japanese fabrics, and they make quilts that are astonishing for their unique design and superb craftsmanship. Our quilt magazines regularly appear in Japanese. The American quilt is admired worldwide.

The Quilt Encyclopedia Illustrated is an important addition to scholarship. No museum curator, art historian, or quilt collector can be without it. The same clarity of understanding that Carter Houck brings to her every project is evident throughout the text and pictures of this volume. It will also serve as a basic reference book and source of information for the novice in the quilt world for years to come.

Robert Bishop, Director, and Elizabeth Warren, Curator, the Museum of American Folk Art

INTRODUCTION

ABOVE: **A finely quilted and trapuntoed linen cap from eighteenth-century France might have been worn by a child or young woman. The Metropolitan Museum of Art, New York. Gift of Mrs. Gilbert W. Chapman, 1976. 1976.3.5**

BELOW: **Japanese firemen in times past wore protective coats of heavily layered and quilted fabric. This one from the late Edo period (nineteenth century) has an amusing design of rabbits pounding rice and is *sashiko*-quilted — the stitches appearing as tiny dots. Collection of Fifi White**

Mention quilts, and the image that almost immediately springs to mind is of the American pieced, or patchwork, bed quilt. The women of the then-new country certainly took quilting to heart and made it their own indigenous art form, but the roots go back for centuries in Europe, and before that in the countries east of the Mediterranean. Quilts were mentioned as a part of household goods in British writings as early as the end of the thirteenth century. Unfortunately, fabric disintegrates more rapidly than the written word, so actual examples — even the tiniest scraps — of early quilts are hard to find.

Quilting, or the joining together of two layers of fabric with batting (filler) between, had its origins in a time that is impossible to document. It is generally thought to have come, in its decorative form, from Asia to Europe at the time of the Crusades — the eleventh to thirteenth centuries A.D. This theory certainly ties together a lot of loose

ends and seems consistent with any sure knowledge of textiles that has been confirmed by research. There is, for example, a Mongolian quilted carpet, probably made a century or so before the birth of Christ and discovered in 1924 in a tomb. It may have been made for burial or it may have graced the floor of a chieftain's tent in his lifetime. It is now kept in the Institute of the Academy of Science of the USSR in Leningrad.

The theory that quilting traveled from the East to the West gains credibility at every turn. The textile arts were much more highly developed in China and India at a far earlier time than in Europe. The use of silk or cotton made it easier to produce a fine texture, suitable for more sophisticated decoration than was possible with the wool or linen used in medieval Europe. Carvings from early Egypt show heavily padded and decorated garments that could well have been layered and quilted.

One of the great clues to its origins may be the way in which Europeans first used quilting — as padding for metal armor and as armor itself. At the time of the Crusades, armies clanked off to war more or less encased in metal. It is fascinating-looking to us, but certainly must have been as uncomfortable as a personal torture chamber, especially considering that as the men traveled south the climate became hotter. It could then follow that the first Crusader chafing in his metal case soon recognized a possible form of relief in the triple thickness of quilting.

The first bits of any quilting found in

Europe are articles of clothing rather like jackets or undershirts that went next to the body or as covers over the armor. The theory is that worn in either way the quilting helped to absorb the shock of arrows, lances, and later even bullets.

Armor was a fact of life for those who adventured and went into battle well into the period of the exploration of the "new world," and we know that both the metal and the quilted varieties traveled across the ocean. Long after firearms were prevalent, armor was still worn. As the one became more accurate and sophisticated, the other became less useful.

By the seventeenth century, quilted clothing for men, women, and children was common. The fabrics varied according to the wearer's class, the finest being of silk with very fine silk or wool batting. In the eighteenth century, skirts parted in the front to reveal more and more of the elaborate quilted petticoats. Caps, jackets, and vests were quilted, corded, and embroidered in intricate and beautiful patterns.

Little remains beyond the household records and wills of the gentry to say that bed quilts were important at this same time. There are also references to them in literature — with many and varied spellings. Such words as "twylt," "quylt," and "twilt" can be found in early English writings.

An 1859 Merriam-Webster dictionary gives a half-column to "quilt" and "quilting." The list of related European words leaves no doubt as to how widespread the knowledge of quilting was. The words cited are: Italian — *coltre*, Latin — *culcita*, Spanish — *colcha*, and Irish — *cuilt*. In any of its forms, the word seems always to have

referred to a layered mattress or bedcover.

During the nineteenth and twentieth centuries, America was the country that kept quilting more than merely alive. It became an art form that changed and was elaborated, a part of women's lives in every stratum of society. While some quilting was done in England and in the Orient, in America it blossomed. Now, toward the end of the twentieth century, it has spread worldwide and has taken on new meanings for each country. More than anything, it forms an artistic bond between women who do not even speak a common language.

C.H.

Appliqué and stuffed-work Bouquet with Trees and Vines, attributed to Virginia Mason Ivey, born 1828 in Kentucky, maker of the famous Kentucky Fair Quilt. Original design and fine workmanship of this type displayed the needlework training given to young girls and women in post-Colonial America. 92 x 78″. Collection of America Hurrah, New York City

ABSTRACT DESIGNS

Many decorative designs are purely abstract, making no attempt to represent anything in nature, but only to be pleasant in terms of arrangement and color. Even though intriguing names like Boston Commons and Wild Goose Chase are attached to some well-known quilt designs, it would take real imagination to make a connection to something recognizable. A number of recent art quilts borrow much of their form and excitement from twentieth-century abstract painting.

See also: Art quilts, Semiabstract designs

AFRICAN-AMERICAN QUILTS

Quilts made by African-Americans are not necessarily identifiable as such. There is, however, a strain of vivid colors and bold geometric designs, reminiscent of African textiles, that runs through many quilts made by black women. With the exception of slave-made quilts, used by the families of the makers' masters, few pieces exist from before the Civil War.

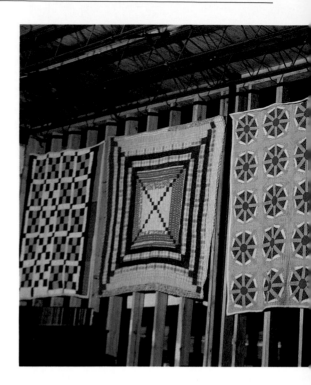

PREVIOUS SPREAD: The Shelburne Museum in Shelburne, Vermont, displays a great number of quilts from its vast collection at all times. On the left is a Sunburst and Sawtooth, pieced by Mrs. Eunice Baker Willard of Castleton, Vermont, in 1860. In the center is a Mariner's Compass, probably made in New Jersey, that won first prize in the 1949 Tennessee State Fair. On the right is an appliqué called Pine Tree, Coxcomb, and Four-Leaf Clover, made in the mid-nineteenth century. Courtesy of the Shelburne Museum, Shelburne, Vermont

RIGHT: The Road Less Traveled by Suzanne Kjelland, inspired by the book of that name, is an abstract interpretation of its theme. The artist dyes her own fabrics to achieve the delicate shading

Two types of African-American quilts dating from the late nineteenth century are still found today in black communities. Beside the aforementioned geometrics, there are story quilts — the best-known of these being the Bible quilts made in the latter half of the nineteenth century by Harriet Powers, a freedwoman. Standard patterns such as stars and Wedding Rings appear in African-American quilts, which are often distinctive for their unique coloring and proportion. Medallion formats were also popular, as was a type of strong strippy arrangement.

See also: Slave-made quilts, Story quilts

ALBUM QUILTS

These are also called "autograph" or "friendship" quilts. Generally, all album quilts are made in blocks, or at least in some separate sections. The blocks are frequently created by a number of people and in different designs. Sometimes one person plans

the overall design and hands out the fabric and pattern or patterns. Often, each block is signed by the person making it — there are very specific patterns that lend themselves to this purpose, blocks having open white spaces in the center, as in Chimney Sweep. When all the blocks are completed, they are often stitched together by the participants in an album party, at which time they would probably be quilted also.

Among the most famous album quilts are those made by a group of women living in the Baltimore area in the midnineteenth century. It is clear that some of these Baltimore album quilts were made by people of differing abilities, while others appear to have been made by one skilled woman. Now that patterns are once again available for these beautiful blocks, many highly skilled quilters make a Baltimore album quilt as a sort of postgraduate appliqué piece. The rules for and definition of an album quilt have always been indefinite, and

the idea has changed with time, so that several varieties of block quilts are now referred to as "album" quilts.

See also: Autograph quilts, Brides' quilts, Freedom quilts, Marriage quilts, Presentation quilts, Sampler quilts, Signature quilts, Wedding quilts

ALL-WHITE QUILTS

The handsome quilts decorated only with intricately quilted designs, usually in white thread on white fabric, have a long history. The earliest-known European quilts and quilted clothing are made with this technique. Petticoats, hats, and bedcovers show off this special and demanding stitchery.

There are many variations on all-white quilts — for example, the patterns are sometimes stuffed to achieve a raised effect. Sometimes only cording is used between

LEFT: The Smith Robertson Museum and Cultural Center in Jackson, Mississippi, is dedicated to the African-American culture of the region. A growing collection of African-American quilts is often on display. Collection of the Smith Robertson Museum, Jackson, Mississippi

BELOW: On the bed is Sunburst by Hystercine Rankin, a well-known African-American quilter from Mississippi. The Jacob's Ladder variation on the wall was made by a neighbor, Thelma Rankin Private collection

Album quilt, signed "Sarah Ann Wilson" and dated 1854. It was probably from a black family since the black figures were not caricatured as was usually the case in quilts by white makers at this time. Research and comparison suggest that this quilt was made by a former slave, perhaps a dressmaker. 85 x 100". Collection of America Hurrah, New York City

the fabric layers, along with thin batting, to emphasize parts of the design.

A variety of fabrics — silk, linen, wool, and cotton — have been used in these elegant quilts. They are also called "whole-cloth" quilts and can be made with top and bottom of two different colors, often so expertly stitched that the quilt is reversible.

See also: Clothing, Corded quilting, Marseilles spreads, Stuffed work, Whole-cloth quilts

ALPHABET QUILTS

Block-like pieced letters — the whole alphabet — have been much used for children's quilts throughout the twentieth century. A well-known pattern of this type was produced by the Ladies' Art Company of St. Louis, Missouri. There have been other alphabet designs for appliqué and embroidery, showing not only the letters but also the usual objects found in an ABC book —

apple for A, and so on. The Nancy Page Quilt Club patterns for such a quilt came out in a newspaper, one letter per week, to whet the quilters' appetites and keep them buying the paper.

See also: Newspaper patterns

AMERICAN QUILTS

It is not unusual to hear the phrase, "American quilts." It would be hard to pin down the exact definition of an American quilt today, although up to at least 1970 there were very distinct differences between American, English, and Welsh quilts. As communication among quilters the world over has improved, the differences are beginning to blur. For purposes of simplification let it be said that America's great contribution to quilting has been the repeating block patterns.

Before block patterns began to be used in American quilts, some characteristic details emerged in what had been essentially English and Welsh designs. After the Revo-

lution, eagles appeared as a frequent design element in medallion and chintz quilts. The fabrics were often of American design, while the album quilts of the second quarter of the nineteenth century were an out-and-out American innovation.

Geometric pieced-block designs grew in popularity after the middle of the nineteenth century, and in the twentieth, swept the country as a craze. Many of the designs related to states and areas and are entirely American in appearance and name.

See also: Baltimore album quilts, Blocks, English quilts, Welsh quilts

AMISH QUILTS

The people in the Amish communities of Pennsylvania, Ohio, and Indiana live as

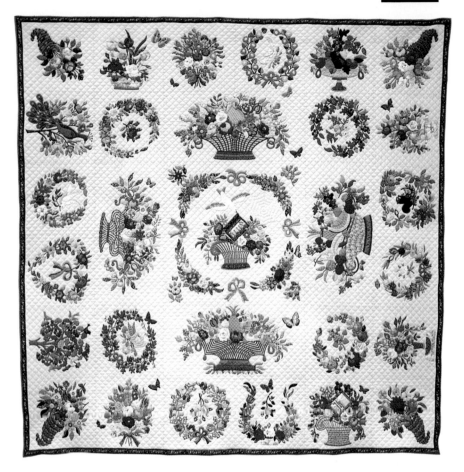

ABOVE: Album quilt, designed and completed by Bernice Enyeart of Huntington, Indiana, in 1985. A modern version of a Baltimore album quilt, its planning and completion required more than three years, although it was not the sole output of the maker during that time. 98 x 98"

LEFT: An alphabet quilt apparently made from the Ladies Art Company patterns in the 1928 catalogue. 87 x 74". Collection of Thos. K. Woodard: American Antiques & Quilts

RIGHT: **North Carolina Lily was made by Nancy Elizabeth Nelson of Pitt County, North Carolina, in the last quarter of the nineteenth century. Such traditional pieced-block patterns, elaborated and enhanced with interesting settings, sashes, corner blocks, and borders are probably the most typical American quilts. 88 x 88". Private collection**

OPPOSITE: **An Indiana Amish quilt made in 1910 uses lighter and brighter colors than are customary in Amish quilts. The Tumbling Blocks pattern is a popular design among Amish of all regions. 82 x 67". Collection of the Museum of American Folk Art, New York. Gift of David Pottinger**

BOTTOM: **Storyteller by Gail Garber of Rio Rancho, New Mexico, is an American quilt inspired by an Indian pottery design. It is shown on a hogan, an adobe dwelling**

nearly in the manner of their grandparents and great-grandparents as possible. Their plain, dark clothing, their bonnets, and their buggies look as though they had never left the nineteenth century. Unfortunately, the true Amish quilts, geometrically pieced and handsomely quilted, are a thing of the past. Most Amish women now make "modern" quilts for sale and for their charity auctions.

The boldly designed, solid-color, pieced quilts that are now so highly favored by collectors were made from the midnineteenth century until about the time of World War

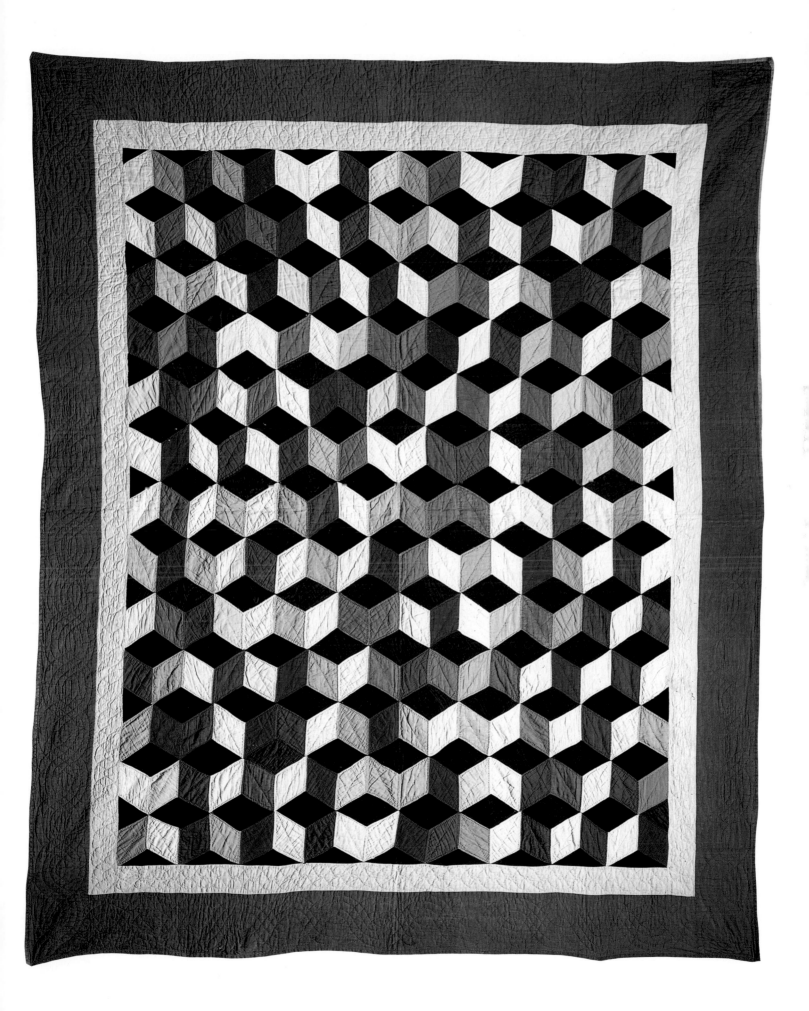

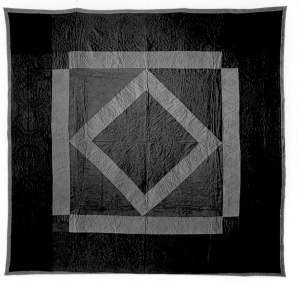

ABOVE: Ohio Amish quilts are often made of wool in a traditional block design. This Ohio Star was made prior to 1920. 72 x 60″. Collection of the Museum of American Folk Art, New York. Gift of David Pottinger

RIGHT: Large, simple center designs, such as Center Diamond, are typical of Lancaster Amish quilts. This one made of wool is dated 1910. 84 x 80″. Collection of the Museum of American Folk Art, New York. Gift of Paige Rense

II, though there are few available from before the turn of the century. They were made to be used, and eventually they wore out. In 1971 Jonathan Holstein mounted the now-famous show "Abstract Design in American Quilts" at the Whitney Museum in New York. In that show were several Amish quilts, most of them from Pennsylvania.

Since that time, Amish quilts have become more popular with collectors than any other type, and have become increasingly hard to find on the open market. The Ohio and Indiana Amish quilts are somewhat similar, using many block patterns popular among the "English," as they call

their non-Amish neighbors. The Pennsylvania Amish quilts are those now-familiar, large Center Diamond and Bars designs, as well as some with smaller, less bold designs such as Sunshine and Shadow.

Darwin Bearley of Akron, Ohio, has collected, studied, and catalogued the Amish quilts of that state, selling some of them to other collectors and dealers. At the same time David Pottinger not only collected Amish quilts in Indiana but gave up his business and moved to the Amish farm area in the northern part of that state. The Indiana State Museum in Indianapolis has bought a large part of his collection and has been displaying and touring small shows around the country so that the general public will be able to see the quilts of the Indiana Amish.

See also: Mennonite quilts, Pieced quilts

ANIMAL MOTIFS

Animals are probably second only to flowers as a subject of designs for quilts, especially children's quilts. Birds have long appeared in both realistic and abstract forms — real-

istic eagles or triangles representing birds on the wing. Cats, dogs, and horses were favorite subjects for appliqué and embroidery in the latter half of the nineteenth century. In the heyday of quilt patterns, cats and dogs appeared in pieced form.

See also: Design sources, Patterns

APPLIQUÉ

Fabric designs cut out of one cloth and stitched or otherwise applied to a contrasting fabric are called by the French word *appliqué*. Examples of such surface enhancement can be found in almost all parts of the world and as far back in history as fabric itself — long before the term was used to define it. When fine print fabrics became generally available in Europe, appliqué became a popular decoration for all sorts of household goods. Quilts with ornate appliqué designs of flowers, birds, and trees were made in both England and America as early as the late eighteenth century.

The actual process of applying one fabric to another in such intricate designs is delicate and painstaking. The edges of each

Circus quilt with pieced animals, from Gilmer, Texas, 1910. A variety of patterns for pieced animals, notably the Kansas City *Star*'s Republican elephant and Democratic donkey, appeared later than these examples, though there may have been commercial patterns even at this date. 47 x 61". Collection of Karey Patterson Bresenhan

Animals were especially popular motifs for quilts at the turn of the century. This one was almost surely made for a child — the top and bottom edges show signs of hard wear. 74 x 62″. Collection of the American Museum in Britain, Claverton Manor, Bath, England

Several newer types of appliqué have taken their place in the American repertory. Reverse appliqué can be considered a simpler form of the process used in the multi-layered mola art of the Cuna-Cuna Indians of the San Blas Islands, off Panama's Caribbean coast. It is also closely related to the intricate two- and three-tone designs of the Hmong people, recently arrived from southeast Asia. The large, continuous "paper-fold" technique from Hawaii is now familiar in all of America and is being employed by quilters everywhere.

See also: Hawaiian quilts, Hmong needlework, Molas, Reverse appliqué

APPRAISALS

Now that quilts have become collectibles, sold at high prices, they must be evaluated, or appraised. Fine modern art quilts and family heirlooms alike should be insured, especially if they are to be shipped to shows and museums. Dealers and auction houses are now competent to determine the value of a fine quilt in greater numbers than they were even ten years ago. There are also appraisal days held at many large quilt shows and at museums. The fee is usually small and the added security is well worth the trouble.

See also: Dating textiles, Documentation

ARMOR

The idea of quilted armor for a soldier is not as odd as it sounds. It made its appearance in Europe at about the time of the early Crusades — the eleventh to thirteenth centuries. References to such cloth armor date to the sixteenth century and some actual pieces from that period can be found in

small piece must be turned under and held in place with tiny stitches. Sometimes a buttonhole or embroidery stitch is used; usually the stitches are "blind," that is, invisible.

Ever since sewing machines were invented in the midnineteenth century, people have tried to use them on appliqué. Until the zigzag machine came into general use after World War II, the only way to do this was to turn the edges under and stitch close to the turned edge, the stitches showing on the surface. Very fine appliqué quilts from as early as 1855, with tiny machine stitches around each appliquéd piece, can still be seen in museums. Zigzag stitching creates a distinct look of its own that adds to the surface texture of the design and is effective in artistic wall hangings and in children's quilts, especially.

LEFT: Whig Rose, Pennsylvania, 1870. Floral appliqué quilts with a great deal of white space for quilting and a well-planned appliqué border were popular in Ohio and Pennsylvania in the nineteenth century, especially in the third quarter. The centers usually consisted of four large blocks set straight or, like this one, five blocks set diagonally. 96 x 95″. Collection of the Museum of American Folk Art, New York. Gift of Karen and Warren Gundersheimer

ABOVE: The first use of quilting in Europe may have been for armor. This sixteenth-century English jack has plates of iron between two layers of canvas (probably linen). The Metropolitan Museum of Art, New York. The Bashford Dean Memorial Collection. Purchase funds from several donors, 1929. 29.158.173

BELOW: Butterfly wall hanging, designed and made by Diane Lane of Wichita, Kansas, 1986. The art of very fine stitchery is as evident in the work of today's best appliqué artists as it was at its height in the 1840s. 18 x 14″. Collection of the author

several collections. The piece most often seen is the jack, or jerkin. It may be made of thickly padded, traditional quilting with heavy linen or canvas outer layers, or it may have small disks of metal stitched between the layers.

Considering the discomfort of metal armor, the idea of a quilted undergarment seems natural, but this was not necessarily the way in which it was used. The jack might have been worn alone or it might have served as a covering for the metal armor. In the days of lances and swords it

Historic Lansing, commissioned from textile artist Jacquelyn Faulkner for the Lansing Centers

LEFT: Founding of the City. Lansing in the mid-1800s includes views of the first capitol dome, the farms and buildings of Michigan Agricultural College, and the railroads of the 1860s. 3 x 7″

LEFT, CENTER: Industrialization of the City: The industrialization of Lansing, exemplified by an assembly line of identical Oldsmobile Curved-dash Runabouts produced from 1900-4. 4 x 7″

would certainly have helped deflect blows, but when guns and cannon took over, its popularity waned with its efficacy.

In the time of armor every person must, of necessity, have been a craftsman of sorts, used to working with his hands. It is not inconceivable that a young man might stitch together his own jerkin. It is also rather appealing to think of his true love quilting this sturdy protective garment before she sent her hero off to battle.

See also: Quilting, Whole-cloth quilts

ART QUILTS

It is possible to date the revival of quilting in America by the 1976 Bicentennial. At about that time the term "contemporary quilt" came into use to describe a new, col-orful, and strikingly artistic quilt and to distinguish it from the lovely traditional quilts that were also a part of that revival. For a while it was easy to understand what was meant by the term, but as time went on, it became apparent that not only was a new form of quilting design emerging, but that it was destined to stay and to change and develop endlessly. Suddenly such quilts could no longer be defined by "contemporary" or "modern" or bracketed by time. It was obvious that fabric was being used to create ever-changing designs, to express ideas, and to do almost everything that could be done with paint on canvas. The art quilt had come of age.

See also: Abstract designs, Quiltmakers (late twentieth century), Semiabstract designs

AUTOGRAPH QUILTS

Many quilts with signed blocks were and are made as gifts for a bride, a person leaving the community, or someone being honored, for any reason. The style of block used is often chosen because of the open space in the center — such designs as Autograph Star or the old favorite, Chimney Sweep — permitting the signer to add a small verse or thought along with the name.

On some of these quilts each person has made and signed her own block but often only a few people — or even one person — have made all the blocks. The signers may be men or other nonsewing members of the community, so autograph quilts vary considerably in the number and origins of their signatures. The terms "album," "auto-graph," and "signature" overlap and are used interchangeably. The fund-raiser is a type of signed quilt that can usually be identified by the enormous number of signatures and the addition of the name of a church or charity. Most signatures on any of these quilts are written in indelible ink and sometimes worked over in embroidery, usually by one skilled person.

See also: Album quilts, Brides' quilts, Freedom quilts, Fund-raiser quilts, Marriage quilts, Presentation quilts, Signature quilts

RIGHT, CENTER: Municipal Development: Carnegie Library, the Post Office, Moores Park Pool, early city buildings, utilities, and roadworks all appear here. 5 x 7"

RIGHT: Aerial Night View: The City, revealed from the air at night by lights and reflections. With the State Capitol and surrounding buildings in the foreground, the city spreads into a pattern of dots and dashes at its perimeter. 9 x 7"

LEFT: **Bittersweet XII** by Nancy Crow of Ohio, made in 1980, brought recognition to quilts as art and to Nancy Crow as one of the leading contemporary quilt artists. She continues to produce her strong original pieces and to lead the way for other textile artists. 82 x 82″. Collection of the Museum of American Folk Art, New York. Gift of the artist

RIGHT: **Chimney Sweep** autograph quilt shown in the Peter Matteson Tavern in Bennington, where it was found in the early twentieth century. Lady Gosford owned the tavern for several years, during which time many people, including Dorothy Canfield Fisher and Norman Rockwell, signed the quilt. She donated both the tavern and the quilt to the Bennington Museum. Collection of the Bennington Museum, Bennington, Vermont

BOTTOM: **Autograph Star** from the midnineteenth century bears the names of many Pennsylvania families, some known to be Quakers, among them Savery, Scattergood, and Wyn. This pattern and the Chimney Sweep pattern remain popular for autograph quilts today. 83 x 79″. Collection of the Museum of American Folk Art, New York. Gift of C. and M. O'Neil

ACKINGS

Quilts are made in three layers. The top layer is usually decorated in some way (appliqué, embroidery, or piecing), the batting or filler for warmth comes next, and the backing, usually a piece of plain fabric, white or colored, seamed as necessary to make it large enough, finishes the quilt. Long ago the backing was coarse homespun, but after the advent of easily available, factory-made goods, the reverse side of quilts became more interesting. In the latter half of the nineteenth century it was not unusual to have backings of extravagantly printed fabrics — perhaps too showy for use anywhere else and therefore bought at a bargain price. Today, prints are also often used.

English quilts were often two-sided, with both a top and backing pieced. This frugal habit, which permitted reversing the cover and having two for the price of one, also appears in some American quilts. In rural areas, plain white feed sacks and other fabric commodity containers were used for back-

ing. Such backs had a number of seams, as each bag provided only about one and a quarter yards of thirty-five-inch or forty-five-inch fabric. To the delight of researchers in later years, the original printed labels did not wash out, giving extra clues to the origins and dates of the quilts.

See also: Batting, Putting In, Tops

BALTIMORE ALBUM QUILTS

Baltimore album quilts are and have been of special significance and of great interest to researchers, collectors, and museums. Album quilts in general became popular about 1840 — the elaborate Baltimore ones were made for the most part in the next decade.

In all current writing about Baltimore album quilts two names appear — Achsah

ABOVE: Baltimore album quilt top (not quilted), attributed to Mary Evans, 1849-52. The designs in appliqué, embroidery, and India ink — baskets, birds, fruit, flowers, cornucopias — are typical of these quilts, sometimes called Baltimore brides' quilts. 109 x 105". Collection of the Museum of American Folk Art, New York. Gift of Mr. & Mrs. James O. Keene

BELOW: Many quilts are backed with whatever fabrics were available, including white cotton sacking used to ship grain or other commodities. This is the back of the cranberry-and-blue Octagon quilt on p.81. Collection of the author

Banners from The Ribbon: A Celebration of Life. Each segment was made by an individual or a group from all over the world, and the entire piece was long enough to wrap the Pentagon. 14 x 28″

BANNERS

Decorated cloth standards, or banners, have existed since they were carried by the knights of medieval Europe marching into battle. In more recent times they have been displayed by political groups, school teams, and in churches. Lately, quilted banners have in many cases replaced the felt ones used for many years. Quilters, who have espoused a number of causes, have created exciting banners for them.

See also: Cause quilts

BASKETS

The use of baskets in everyday life and their engagingly simple shapes make them perfect motifs for quilt design. They can be filled with flowers and fruits or left starkly plain. Country basket designs, pieced with triangles to fit the confines of a block, have been made in both England and America. for at least two hundred years. The elaborate appliqué Baltimore baskets created by Mary Evans Ford for her quilts remain a staple of quiltmaking to this day.

The flood of new block designs created for the early-twentieth-century pattern companies and the ever-popular offerings in newspapers brought out still more basket patterns. Some of these were large, simple appliqué designs and some were elaborations of the pieced baskets that had been around for more than a century. There was a constantly increasing selection of flower, fruit, and bird images to be used with the baskets. In some cases these were published one at a time, like the alphabet designs, so that by the time a quilter had collected all of them, she could make a large basket sampler quilt.

See also: Baltimore album quilts

Goodwin Wilkins and Mary Evans Ford. The connection of both women with Methodism and the impression that many of the quilts were group efforts make it highly probable that they were created by church sewing circles. Some few seem to have come from one extremely skilled hand and are believed to be the expert work of Mary Evans Ford alone.

A number of these beautiful pieces are now in museums and private collections. Their longevity is probably due to the fine fabrics used and to the fact that since they were made as presentation or brides' quilts, they would have been used only as elegant spreads for best beds rather than as everyday covers needed for warmth.

The intricate designs of baskets and bouquets have so caught the imagination of today's fine quilters that there is a renaissance of this type of quilt. New designs, patterns, and books are leading the way to twentieth-century Baltimore quilts.

See also: Album quilts, Brides' quilts, Presentation quilts

BATTING

A true quilt is three-layered, the middle layer being a soft fluffy filler, or batting, for warmth. The batting is held in place between the backing and the decorated top by the quilting stitches, which go through all layers.

Before the midnineteenth century, batting was simply loose fibers carded and spread by hand flatly onto the backing before the top was smoothed over it — like the filling in a sandwich. Cotton and wool were the most generally available fibers and could be distributed evenly without pulling apart.

The earliest commercial batting sold in America, Stearns & Foster's Mountain Mist, first appeared in 1846. From that time on, cotton batting, rolled and wrapped, was available in dry-goods stores. That does not mean that everyone who quilted purchased ready-made batting. It was more economical to use not only raw cotton or wool, but also worn blankets, flannel sheets, and even tattered quilts. It is not unusual to pull away the outer layer of a lumpy country quilt and find another pieced quilt between the layers.

Today's quilter has a wide choice of bat-tings, to be purchased packaged or by the yard. Pure cotton or wool is still available. Silk batting is imported from the Orient and is perfect for use in quilted clothing. Polyester and cotton-poly mixtures are favored by some quilters for their washabili-ty and long-wearing qualities.

Some types of quilts have no batting — most of the silk and velvet Victorian quilts were made as throws for the sofa and usually consisted only of a top and backing. There are some fancy cotton pieces, generally decorated with appliqué, that look exactly like quilts, except that they have no batting and no quilting. These are called, variously, spreads, coverlets, and summer coverlets. *See also: Backings, Coverlets, Putting In, Spreads, Summer Coverlets, Throws, Tops*

LEFT: A close-up detail of quilt batting layered between the top and back-ing of a whole-cloth quilt. The backing and batting will be trimmed even with the top before the edge is bound. Courtesy of Fairfield Processing Corp.

RIGHT: Basket of Scraps, also known as Cactus Bas-ket, late nineteenth century, Missouri. The precise piec-ing and arrangement, as well as the simple border, are typical of quilts of the period and area. Collection of Dick and Suellen Meyer

RIGHT: **A quilting bee in a private home in North Dakota, ca. 1885. When not in use, the quilt frame would be hoisted to the ceiling on the cords at the two back corners and fastened through loops or with screen-door hooks on the front corners. North Dakota State Historical Society, Bismark, North Dakota**

BELOW: **The dove is a favorite Biblical motif, translated into another of the many Drunkard's Path or Robbing Peter to Pay Paul quilt designs. The quilt was made by Suzzy Chalfant Payne and Susan Aylsworth Murwin**

BEES

Quilting bees are meetings of people gathered for the purpose of quilting and finishing tops that were made by one of the members of the bee or by an outsider who needs this assistance or service for any of a number of reasons. A group of this kind was referred to as late as 1859 in the Merriam-Webster dictionary as a "quilting." In the same dictionary a "bee" was identified as "an assembly of ladies to sew for the poor."

Quilting groups, or bees, still work for "the poor," for children's hospitals or hospices, or for a dozen other charities and causes. Some groups quilt for people who enjoy piecing or otherwise making the tops but prefer to pay to have them quilted. These groups are often church-associated, the money that they earn going to the church. Quilting bees are common now and serve at least three purposes — the purely social enjoyment of getting together, the

finishing of quilts that might not otherwise be finished, and often the making of quilts for money for a favorite charity.

See also: Quilting bees

BIBLE-INSPIRED PATTERNS

In Early American homes, reading material was limited, but the one book that could usually be found was the Bible. Bible stories were told to children from their earliest years, and Biblical names were very much a part of everyday life. As the variety of quilt patterns proliferated, it was natural that many of them should take on names with religious significance.

Among the earliest of these patterns was the Star of Bethlehem, a large and showy arrangement of 45° diamonds. Others were simpler block designs such as Jacob's Ladder, Crown of Thorns, and Hosannah, or The Palms. The favorite appliqué design — in all its many variations — was Rose of Sharon. These Bible-inspired patterns are no less popular today and are often incorporated into presentation quilts for ministers or banners for churches, as well as into family album quilts. There has been at least one very good book devoted to them, *Creative American Quilting Inspired by the Bible*, by Murwin & Payne, unfortunately now out of print, but possibly available in libraries.

See also: Album quilts, Banners, Presentation quilts

BIBLE QUILTS

Bible stories and religious symbols have inspired artists in all media through the ages. Many of the nineteenth-century quilters knew few other stories than those they heard in church and at the family Bible

reading. Adam and Eve, Noah's Ark, and other famous biblical tales are the subjects of a number of quilts. Some have sober designs, others are lighthearted, in the manner of colorful illustrations for children's Bible stories.

See also: Bible-inspired patterns, Religious quilts

Nancy Roan of Boyertown, Pennsylvania, designed and made a full-size Adam and Eve quilt, combining Pennsylvania-German folk art themes with the Biblical story. 78 x 91"

BICENTENNIAL QUILTS

Just as the Centennial year in the nineteenth century brought forth a burst of patriotic enthusiasm, so did the Bicentennial in 1976. Quilting had been almost dormant since World War II, but suddenly women young and old, skilled needlewomen, and those who had never sewed a stitch, began to

The Westport, Connecticut, Bicentennial quilt was a community project, taking two years to complete. Designed by a professional artist, Naiad Einsel, and worked by gifted amateurs, it was overseen by professional quilter Micki McCabe. More than sixty people worked on this project conceived by Margaret C. Henkel. It has remained on public view since the Bicentennial year, 1976. 78 x 105″. Courtesy of Naiad Einsel and the Westport Historical Society

prompted by the new Bicentennial enthusiasm. Old quilts were taken from attic storage, new quilts were made, and guilds were formed. There were predictions that this enthusiasm would be short-lived, but more than ten years later it is obvious that quilting has become a part of the fiber of society. Large annual shows are now established, quilt artists are recognized by museums, and guilds and classes devoted to quiltmaking are a permanent part of most communities.

The quilts that set off this burst of creativity varied from homemade, fabric love letters to America to magnificently designed and executed works of art perfectly planned for public buildings. They are pieced, appliqué, and embroidered. They depict historical events, hope for the future, and love of country. Fortunately, most quilters felt strongly enough about their work to sign and date it so that future historians will be able to understand more about the people who participated in this historical moment. *See also: Centennial quilts, Commemorative quilts*

BINDING

The edges of quilts must be neatly finished in some manner, and binding with fabric is the most common method. In the eighteenth and well into the nineteenth centuries, quilts were often bound with a fine woven tape made on a tape loom. Presumably the maker of the quilt was often the weaver of such tape.

Binding can also be a decoration, carefully planned to carry out a special color scheme. There are two schools of thought about the way in which the binding should be cut — one favors cutting on the straight

design and create fabric posters for the occasion. Women who had always quilted were called into service by groups eager to learn. Artists produced patterns, and work days were set up in libraries, historical societies, and churches so that the quilts could be completed in time to hang for the celebration. Many are still displayed in state capitols, libraries, and other public buildings.

In small towns and large, sophisticated cities there were exhibitions of quilts grain, the other, on the bias. One argument for bias binding is that it can be made double, or "French," and is therefore more durable. The binding on quilts that are entered in judged shows comes in for careful scrutiny. It must be even, lie flat, and have well-turned or carefully rounded corners.

See also: Cording, Edging, Lace, Piping, Ruffles

BISCUIT QUILTS

Among the novelty quilts that have appeared in the twentieth century, the most practical is the Biscuit quilt. It is made up of segments of fabric, each stuffed and completed before being joined to the next piece. The design possibilities are limited, but for a fairly quickly made, warm covering the Biscuit quilt is far superior to its more decorative cousins, the Yo-Yo and the Cathedral Windows. A few talented designers have used some form of this construction in art quilts.

See also: Cathedral Windows, Yo-Yo

BLOCKS

What comes most readily to mind as a quilt block is the pieced square in all its variety. Blocks can, however, be decorated with appliqué or embroidery and then joined together, or "set," as a quilt top. Album quilts and sampler quilts are usually made up in any of several block designs, generally in identical sizes. The most popular size is twelve inches square, probably because it is so easily divided into four, nine, or sixteen squares for further design possibilities. The setting of blocks can be done in many ways, the squares joined to make one large design or separated by strips, further increasing the design options.

The pieced quilt, and especially block

designs, are peculiarly American. Some simple geometric blocks were used mainly on the borders of English quilts, but by the late nineteenth century American women began to elaborate endlessly on the basics. It took little more than a pencil and ruler, or better yet, a square of paper to fold and use as a pattern for a cardboard template, to create a multitude of designs within a simple twelve-inch-square framework. By the twentieth century, many new companies, operating on the premise that not every woman wanted to be her own designer, thrived on printing simple block patterns. It was easy to fit either pieced or appliqué designs of this size into a convenient newspaper format and later onto the pages of a book.

The geometric possibilities of pieced

Mary Pemble Barton's homage to America is this Heritage Quilt which she designed and made. It took ten years to complete the appliqué and piecing. The women of the St. Petri Lutheran Church quilted it in time for the 1976 Bicentennial celebration. The scenes and figures represent the migration of families from the eastern United States, like the maker's own, to Iowa in the midnineteenth century. 101 x 102". Collection of the artist

Typical of the best country quilts of the late nineteenth century is the block design, appliquéd as seen here or pieced, with simple sashes and border. This fine example was made in Pitt County, North Carolina, by Nancy Elizabeth Nelson in the late 1880s. 90 x 90″. Private collection

blocks continue to be endless. The variety of even the most basic collection cannot be covered here, but there are many books available on block designs. Several large specialized dictionaries depict every imaginable design from the past, complete with names and origins.

See also: Corner blocks, Four-patch designs, Nine-patch designs, Pieced quilts, Robbing Peter to Pay Paul, Sashes, Sets

BLOCK-BY-BLOCK QUILTING

The problem of finding enough space to set up a large quilting frame is not new. One solution is to complete each block with batting and backing and quilting, so that no frame is required. The blocks are then joined, the top and batting of one block seamed to the next to make rows. The backing is finished invisibly by hand and then another row joined. Quilts from as early as the midnineteenth century can be found finished in this way. This system is also called "quilt-as-you-go."

See also: Lap quilting, Quilt-as-you-go

BLOCK CONTESTS

A block contest is exactly what the name implies — a contest in which each entrant is to design and make a block of a specified size. When time is short and the intent is to involve as many people as possible, the block contest is the choice of guilds and quilt-show committees, as well as of batting and fabric companies. There is usually a theme — "Garden," "Circus," "Famous Women," or something with local significance. The rules state the subject and exact dimensions (including seam allowance), and any other specific information, such as color and technique.

Winning blocks are chosen, as in any other contest, by judges and a system of elimination. These blocks are usually put together in a quilt with "honorable mention" blocks filling out the format. Many of the finished quilts or wall hangings are donated to hospitals or schools. Those owned by companies are used for publicity.
See also: Blocks, Contests, Sets

BLOCK PRINTING

The earliest-known method of printing designs on fabric is block printing. The design is cut into the smooth surface of a piece of wood or metal, or a thin sheet of metal or felt with the design cut out is glued to wood. The color is applied with a roller or by pressing the block into a dye pad. Covering an entire piece of fabric by this method is obviously laborious and time-consuming, but considered by many the best way of creating a continuous design. The method is not used commercially in this country today, but artisans print on paper with linoleum blocks, and children

are often taught this skill using a potato into which they can easily cut a design.
See also: Copperplate printing, Dyes

BLUE-RIBBON QUILTS

One description that is often used for very fine quilts is, quite naturally, "blue-ribbon." The description should be applied only to those quilts that have actually won top honors in judged shows of some importance. Many shows now have ribbons of other colors, frequently purple, for Best-of-Show, so the term "blue-ribbon" is a little misleading.
See also: Contests, Judged shows, Juried shows, Prizewinning quilts, Shows, State fairs

The thirty winning entries in the Famous Women Block Contest, sponsored in 1978 by Mountain Mist Batting, were joined into a full-size quilt. The portraits represent a wide range of women from Nefertiti and Queen Elizabeth I to Amelia Earhart and Edith Head. 79 x 96″. Courtesy of Mountain Mist Co.

**Snowscape was designed
and made in wool by Jo
Diggs of Maine. At the Vermont Quilt Festival it won a
blue ribbon and a purple
for best-of-show in 1984.
48 x 72″**

BORDERS

Early medallion quilts were almost nothing
but borders, one outside the other around a
center block. Borders remain an essential
part of many quilts and there seem to be
few rules for them that cannot be broken.
Appliqué borders are often used on pieced
quilts, and pieced borders can work well on
appliqué quilts. Borders may be in solid colors and heavily quilted or may be made in
bands of several colors, usually repeating
the colors within the quilt.

The border is an integral part of certain
designs — the Amish Center Diamond is a
good example of this classic arrangement.
Many country quilts, made to be used as
warm bedcovers, were block-pieced and
then bound, with no border. Between these
two extremes, borders are an artistic choice,
planned to enhance the total effect of the
quilt. This means that proportion, color,
and corner treatment must also be carefully
considered.

See also: Amish quilts, Medallion quilts

BRIDES' QUILTS

There are, undoubtedly, many quilts that
have been made for brides but do not appear
in any way to be brides' quilts. There was a
story often told, and possibly somewhat
embellished, about young women in the
eighteenth and nineteenth centuries making

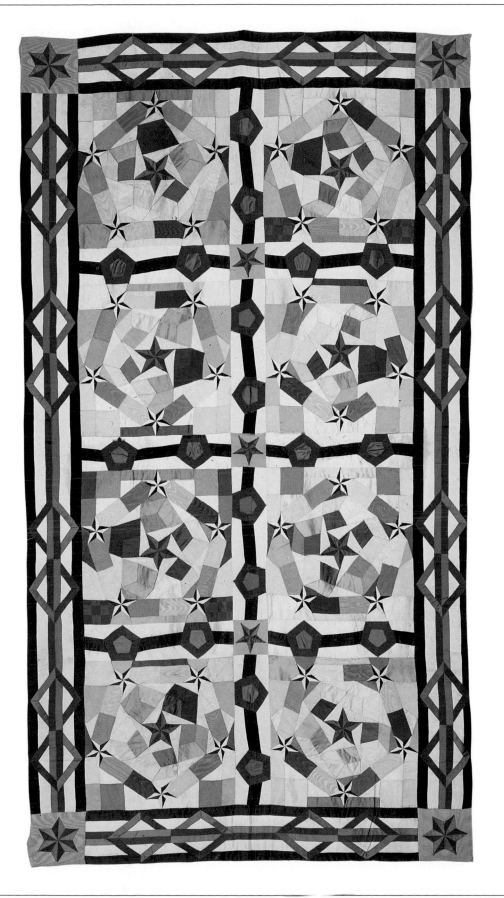

A "contained" crazy quilt is neatly arranged with blocks and sashes and a border conforming perfectly with the interior design and color. The geometry and measurements of the border design were planned with care; the corner blocks carried out the star motif in the blocks. Late nineteenth century, New Hope, Pennsylvania. 80 x 44". Collection of the Museum of American Folk Art, New York. Gift of Jaqueline L. Fowler

A *broderie perse* and stuffed-work quilt from Maryland remains in the family of the maker, Mary Brawner Livers, born 1766. The quilt was probably made in the first two decades of the nineteenth century. Private collection

twelve quilts before they were engaged and then a thirteenth for the marriage bed. Many a young woman certainly worked on her own bride's quilt, alone or with a group of friends. Some brides' quilts were album or friendship quilts, with a variety of blocks made by several people or blocks signed by friends and relatives.

One favorite style for a wedding or bride's quilt has always been the whole-cloth, often with padded or raised designs. The names of the bride and groom and other information can be worked in the center of such a quilt as part of the design.

In this century the Double Wedding Ring has been a favorite bride's quilt. The significance is obvious, and there is also space in

the rings for signatures and dates. Other designs much favored for brides are hearts, flowers (especially roses), and unbroken circles or wreaths.

See also: Album quilts, Baltimore album quilts, Marriage quilts, Wedding Ring quilts

BRODERIE PERSE

A surprisingly large number of quilts and coverlets, both English and American, decorated with this type of cutout appliqué, survive from the late eighteenth and early nineteenth centuries, although the term *broderie perse* did not appear until well after the middle of the nineteenth century.

In *A World of Embroidery*, published in 1975 by Charles Scribner's Sons, Mary Gostelow suggested that the term *broderie perse* ("Persian embroidery") first gained currency in England with the Great Exhibition of 1851 in London's Crystal Palace. At that time all things Eastern or Oriental were very fashionable in both England and America. The French name probably appealed to the public. It is now commonly used to describe delicate cutout designs of print fabric, usually chintz, applied to a solid foundation fabric with fine embroidery stitches. A closely-worked buttonhole stitch was favored, though the edges can be simply turned and blind-stitched, as with any other appliqué. The process seems to have preceded the name.

See also: Appliqué, Chintz, Palampores, Tree of Life

 CALICO

If there is one fabric that is synonymous with quilts it is calico, the ubiquitous printed cotton used over the last two centuries for children's clothes, daytime dresses, blouses, and aprons. The name — also spelled "callicoe" and "calicoe" — came with the original printed cottons from Calicut, India. For more than a century before the roller-printing process was perfected and used in Europe and America, colorful floral cottons were imported into England from India. The designs showed an increasingly strong English influence as the trade grew in the seventeenth century — a case of the product changing to meet the demand.

The base fabric of calico has not always been the same — weaves varied somewhat but were usually smooth, flat ones that accepted printing well. The characteristic that defines calico is that it is printed with multicolored, frequently floral, designs. Fashions in the United States have dictated colors and patterns too numerous to describe. Small floral prints from the late nineteenth century are often easily recognizable, making it possible to date many quilts from that era. On the other hand there were some small designs from that time that continued to be printed late into the twentieth century, and others that have been revived, so that a thorough knowledge of the designs, textures, and dyes is necessary for accurate dating.

The era from 1920 to 1940 saw the largest expansion of cotton prints or calicoes imaginable. The colors were especially fresh and appealing bright pastels. The print designs were so varied — and often

humorous — that it is almost impossible to understand how the time, labor, and talent could have been expended on fabric that sold for a mere nine cents to eighteen cents a yard. During this time home sewing flourished and women made not only quilts but most of the clothing and household items needed in the home, doubtless encouraging great competition in the textile industry for their patronage.

See also: Charm quilts, Copperplate printing, Roller printing

CALIMANCO

All-wool whole-cloth quilts were popular in the eighteenth and early nineteenth centuries. The fabrics were, in general, coarse

Whole-cloth quilt of a highly glazed woolen fabric known as "calimanco," with initials "A.P." and date, "Dec. 1788," worked in quilting across the pillow area. Shown in the Webb House, Wethersfield, Connecticut, in a room with original wallpaper of the same period. Collection of the Webb-Deane-Stevens Museum

Above: Center Square in a Diamond, Leeds County, Ontario, ca. 1825-50. This rough utility quilt of homespun wool and cotton yarns is typical of Canadian quilts throughout the nineteenth century. 60 x 77". The Ruth McKendry Collection, Museum of Civilization, Ontario, Canada

BELOW: Medallion quilt, signed and dated, "Mary Morris aged 14, 1825," from the Elgin area, Leeds County, Ontario, Canada. The early Canadian quilts, like many from the United States, reflect the English background of their makers. 73 x 79". The Ruth McKendry Collection, Museum of Civilization, Canada

and rough-finished, though some were glazed by a process of heat and pressure. One name for this type of smoother, more elegant wool was "calimanco." The glaze and the colors remain surprisingly clear and bright in many of these quilts after two hundred years or more.

See also: Glazed fabrics, Linsey-woolsey, Whole-cloth quilts

CANADIAN QUILTS

Much of Canada was settled by people from the British Isles similar to those who settled the United States to the south. They brought with them the same inheritance of quilts and quilting. The large French population made woven bedcovers but seems to have added nothing to the quilts of Canada. The art evolved differently in the two countries, although there was communication and some exchange of population, so that new patterns did cross the border.

The largest number of existing antique Canadian quilts are pieced and many are fairly simple, made primarily for warmth. Museums contain some appliqué, many made as marriage quilts and some for grander houses with a more leisurely way of life. It stands to reason that in a cold northern country more people would make warm utility quilts than any other kind. Ruth McKendry, author of *Quilts and Other Bedcoverings in the Canadian Tradition*, says that if she is asked about a uniquely Canadian quilt, one of the bold, colorful, pieced wools comes instantly to mind.

Canada has also experienced a quilting revival in the last quarter of the twentieth century. New books are coming out of that country — both on the subject of their

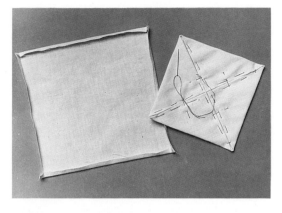

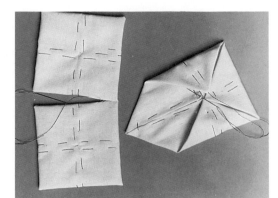

ABOVE, LEFT AND RIGHT: Constructing Cathedral Windows piecing, shown in three steps

BELOW, LEFT: Adding colored squares into the folded muslin pieces to create Cathedral Windows

BELOW, RIGHT: A finished section of Cathedral Windows.

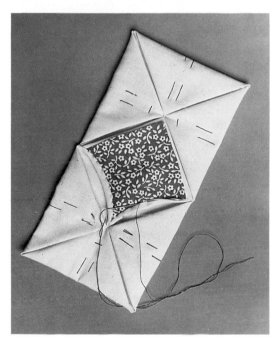

quilting heritage and on the new wave of art quilts. There is a healthy exchange of ideas, designs, and teachers between the United States and Canada. Museums are displaying quilts both old and new, and there is currently strong support for research in the field of quilts in Canada.

See also: Pieced quilts, Utility quilts, Wool

CATHEDRAL WINDOWS

One dictionary of pattern names refers to Cathedral Windows, a folded fabric design, as a "nonquilt" because it has neither batting nor backing. It is a bedspread, or coverlet, made up of squares of fabric — usually muslin — folded to frame other, smaller squares of colored or print fabric. The total effect is somewhat like sparkling squares of stained glass.

See also: Yo-Yo

CAUSE QUILTS

The making of a quilt has often been at the same time the making of a statement that is undoubtedly a strongly held belief, sometimes political and almost always emotional.

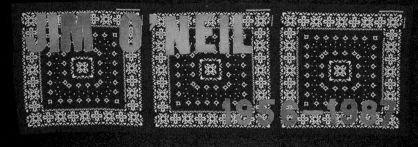

The AIDS Memorial Quilt, capable of covering fourteen acres, is a sixteen-ton patchwork of 3-by-6-foot panels commemorating those who have died of AIDS. A large section is shown here spread on the Capitol Mall in Washington, D.C. Shown below are details of panels. Courtesy of the NAMES Project

In a sense, many quilts listed in other ways also could be listed as cause quilts. A quilt made to celebrate a national milestone such as the Centennial or Bicentennial, or one made to mourn the loss of a loved one, or one made to express patriotism in wartime may also be called a cause quilt. In recent times the causes of peace, homelessness, and child abuse have all been subjects for quilt artists. The AIDS Memorial Quilt, displayed for the last time in Washington, D.C., in 1989, and made of panels created by relatives and friends of victims of the disease, weighed sixteen tons and included

10,848 commemorative panels.

See also: Bicentennial quilts, Centennial quilts, Patriotic quilts, Political quilts, Protest quilts, War quilts

CELTIC QUILTS

Designs from many ancient cultures have been translated into quilts and quilting. Among the most appropriate and lasting are the great Celtic designs, seen in metalwork from the Celtic Golden Age — the seventh to the ninth centuries A.D. — and thought to have been used as early as the fourth century in other artifacts. These designs are evident in the Welsh all-white quilts and in the few Irish wool quilts that have survived.

During the late-twentieth-century revival of quilting in America two Irish-born women turned back to Celtic designs for quilting almost simultaneously. Philomena Wiechec approached it as appliqué, using fine folds of bias-cut fabric. Mary Butler Shannon used the designs, as her forebears had, in elaborately beautiful quilting compositions. The two approaches have merged and the result may be seen in many pieces by both women and by the hundreds of people they have taught.

See also: Irish quilts, Welsh quilts

CENTENNIAL QUILTS

Quilters have always used their art to celebrate occasions and to proclaim their patriotism. 1876 was already a high point for quilting and needlework of all kinds, so women were able to celebrate the Centennial of the United States in a burst of creative enthusiasm. There were fabrics printed with flags, national heroes, public buildings, and even the date. Many of these were used in Centennial quilts, along with historic scenes and patriotic mottoes. A hundred years later, the Bicentennial was responsible for a rebirth of quilting.

See also: Bicentennial quilts, Patriotic quilts

CHALLENGES

Quilters never tire of competition, and the most recent type, perfectly suited to groups and guilds, is the "challenge." The rules for this type of contest have very narrow guidelines, often including the use of several specific fabrics. For example, five coordinated fabrics will be chosen and the rules will

state that each competitor must use at least three of these, though she may add three to five more fabrics of her own choice. It may also be stated that the competition pieces must be of a certain size and must be pieced, or whatever other specifications the committee decides upon.

See also: Contests, Judged shows

ABOVE: There is no doubt that this quilt was made by G. Knappenberger to celebrate the Centennial in 1876. It is interesting that there are no patriotic symbols, no flags, no Americana other than the traditional designs found in many earlier American quilts. 83 x 71″. Collection of the Museum of American Folk Art, New York. Gift of Rhea Goodman

LEFT: This Celtic sampler, made by Donna Stout of Ontario, Canada, is from Philomena Wiechec's *Celtic Quilt Designs* book. The setting is a Garden Maze

RIGHT: This quilt, made in 1876 by a member of the Burdick-Child family, North Adams, Massachusetts, has a block (second from the left in the top row) that probably depicts Memorial Hall at the Centennial International Exposition held in Philadelphia. Many of the other blocks are humorous and anecdotal, a view of one family's life at the time of the Centennial. 78 x 79". Courtesy of the Shelburne Museum, Shelburne, Vermont

BELOW: The Other Side of Charm by Patricia Cox is made up of what she calls "flip-flop" pieces, each section being a mirror image of another piece. No two pieces of fabric are alike, making it a charm quilt. 36" across

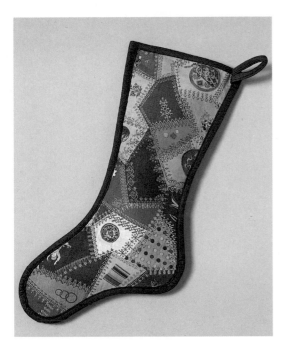

CHARM QUILTS

Quilters have always enjoyed thinking up new ways to make quilts — often based on old ideas or patterns. In the late nineteenth century, charm quilts were invented and quickly became popular. The rules are that there may be no identical fabrics in the quilt. The same print in different colors may be used, but no closer similarity is permissible. The most favored patterns for charm quilts are the compelling geometric one-patch designs like Tumbling Blocks, Postage Stamp, and hexagons.

Fabric for charm quilts is usually collected from fellow quilters, remnant sales, and friends and family for the quilts that will become keepsakes. The fabrics of choice are washable cottons, preferably calico prints, though in Victorian times some quilts were made of silk and velvet. The challenge lies in putting a variety of fabrics together so that they blend well and create a totally coordinated effect.

See also: Calico, One-patch designs

CHEATER CLOTH

The manufacturers of calico or other cotton print fabrics have always been attuned to the needs of quilters. Not only do they print a wonderful array of designs and colors to be pieced into the many patterns known and catalogued, but they have perceived the need for fabrics that imitate pieced quilt tops. It is possible to buy stars, Log Cabins, and even crazy quilts, apparently already pieced, but in actuality simply printed to look surprisingly authentic. The logical name for these ingenious fakes is "cheater cloth." Such shortcut fabrics are especially useful for baby quilts, toys, table mats, and other quick gift items.

See also: Crazy quilts, Pieced quilts

CHILDREN'S QUILTS

Even the most serious quilters like to work in amusing styles and with designs taken from everyday life. One of the best outlets for such a happy form of quilting is a quilt for a child. If it is made for a bed rather

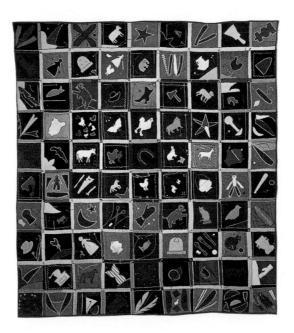

LEFT: A cheater cloth version of Victorian crazy quilting is perfect for making a Christmas stocking. Collection of Patricia Cox

BELOW: This early twentieth century quilt appears to have been made not only for but at least partially by a child. The fabrics, mostly flannel, are enhanced with simple embroidery stitches. 69 x 62″. Collection of Thos. K. Woodard: American Antiques & Quilts

A quilt with appliquéd chintz cutouts is typical of both English and American work of the late eighteenth and early nineteenth centuries. This piece is from either the Adams or Boyce family of Laurens County, South Carolina, ca. 1825. 96 x 86″. Collection of the D.A.R. Museum, Washington, D.C. 83.33

than a cradle or crib, it can be stronger and more brilliant in theme and color and can be enjoyed longer. Sometimes a child's quilt is made as a wall decoration, and the child can take it through life.

See also: Alphabet quilts, Cradle quilts, Crib quilts, Juvenile quilts

CHINTZ

We know chintz as a floral printed fabric with a repeat pattern, usually with a glazed or polished finish. It has been used since Colonial times in home furnishings, and is seen in many of the late-eighteenth- and early-nineteenth-century quilts, both English and American. The palampore panels in Tree of Life quilts and many of the other appliqué designs were made of chintz.

It was also used in pieced borders in the elegant medallion quilts of those earlier centuries.

The history of chintz (spelled "chints" in early records) goes back as far as the first trade routes from India and the East. In the seventeenth century it was imported into England, where it became very popular and the designs slowly became influenced by the English to suit their tastes. The printing process is described as "painted and printed," which suggests that chintz was designed and made with great skill and was available only to the wealthy classes. Though it continues to be more expensive than many other cotton prints, very high-quality chintz is now manufactured in England and America and is still used as a furnishing fabric and sometimes in quilts.

See also: Broderie perse, Palampores, Tree of Life

CIGAR BAND SILKS

Around the turn of the century it was a mark of gentlemanly elegance to smoke cigars — preferably fine, hand-rolled ones. As cellophane had not yet been invented and silk was relatively inexpensive, bundles of fine cigars were wrapped in silk cigar ribbons, measuring up to one and a half inches wide, about eighteen inches long, and printed with the name of the cigar company. They were usually gold in color, occasionally red or white. No woman could possibly let them be discarded at a time when the vogue was for silk quilts in small throw sizes for sofas. The accumulation of enough of these narrow silk bands to create even a fifty-four-inch-square, strip-pieced top seems a small reward for enduring a house filled with cigar smoke!

Quite a few cigar-band quilts exist in museums and private collections, most from between 1890 and 1910. Though the majority are gold-colored, the shades tended to vary with the different companies, so there is enough diversity to make the quilt designs interesting. The printing and the embroidery stitches used to join the bands make attractive patterns of lights and darks.

See also: Tobacco premiums, Victorian crazy quilts

CIGARETTE PREMIUMS

In the early twentieth century there appears to have been a conscious effort on the part of cigarette companies to entice women to smoke. Various premiums were offered, either in the pack itself or through the mail — a number of coupons from the packs paid for each gift.

Cigar band silk quilt or throw, made in 1900 by Sadie Coe. Mrs. Coe's husband collected these bands from stores and hotels as he traveled through the Pacific Northwest. The strips are feather-stitched together in the Victorian style, with a ruffle added to two edges. 55 x 77". Photographed in the Pacific Hotel in historic San José, California. Private collection

One in-pack variety of premium was a small piece of fabric evidently intended for the use of quilters. In some brands this was a flag, usually of a cotton flannel fabric. The object was to collect flags from a variety of countries and sew them together. It took the full number of flags and many duplicates to produce even a throw for the sofa.

The more elegant silk-ribbon pieces were for use in Victorian crazy quilts or pillows. The silk was of the same quality to be found in good ribbon of the period, often with a satin finish and with emblems woven in. They might represent countries or colleges, butterflies or maps and quickly became collectibles, as did the flannel flags. The names of the cigarette companies were prominently displayed — Egyptienne Luxury, Old Mill, or Nebo, for example.

See also: Flag quilts, Tobacco premiums, Victorian crazy quilts

CLOTHING

It is nearly impossible to trace the origins of quilted clothing. It appears in works of art from the Egyptian First Dynasty, more than 3,000 years B.C. Ancient styles of Japanese and Chinese clothes were quilted in numerous ways, some even having geometric patchwork designs, at least in the last five or six centuries and possibly earlier.

Soon after quilting reached Europe,

probably brought from the East by the Crusaders, it was used for both clothing and bedcovers. By the late seventeenth and early eighteenth centuries quilted petticoats were so elaborately decorated that skirts were split in front to show off the fine handwork. Like the all-white quilts, they were made with linen, silk, or cotton on the outside and fine wool batting for warmth and body.

Men and women have worn quilted caps or hats, waistcoats, and jackets, often elaborately stitched and embroidered. By the eighteenth century many of these styles had died out, but quilted jackets keep reappearing in many forms. In the late nineteenth century such frivolous articles as quilted tippets for ladies appeared. In recent years, both quilting and patchwork have been popular in ready-to-wear as well as in clothing designed and made by quilters.

See also: Introduction, All-white quilts, Fashion, Wearable art

COLLECTORS

The few people who saw the value of quilts and started to collect them early in the twentieth century were able to save many pieces that would otherwise have been worn out and destroyed. Luckily they were wise enough to recognize the artistic value of something made essentially for household use. Only in very recent years has the public at large begun to understand the difference between a quilt of important artistic design and a bed covering.

Among the early-twentieth-century collectors of quilts were Ruth Finley, Florence Peto, and Carrie Hall (who collected blocks rather than quilts). Ruth Finley wrote *Old Patchwork Quilts and the Women Who Made Them*, published in 1929. Florence Peto wrote two books and many magazine articles about quilts well into the period after World War II when there were still only a few people interested in making or collecting quilts. Carrie Hall's *The Romance of the Patchwork Quilt*, first published in 1935, shows, in rather poor black-and-white photographs, many of the blocks from her collection. Also shown are whole quilts from other collections, notably those of Charlotte Jane Whitehill, who was also a well-known quiltmaker of the time. Apparently, people who make quilts also become interested in collecting them.

Electra Havemeyer Webb started collecting American folk art with the purchase of a cigar-store Indian in 1907. In the next decades she amassed what remains an outstanding collection that includes hundreds of quilts. In 1952, eight years before her death, she opened the Shelburne Museum in Vermont so that the public could enjoy and understand American folk art. As interest in quilts grew after the Bicentennial, the Shelburne's quilt collection became a magnet for serious students of the art.

Jonathan Holstein and Gail van der Hoof collected pieced quilts — simple, strong, and fascinating for their bold abstract design. In 1971 the Whitney Museum showed this collection under the title "Abstract Design in American Quilts," and the art world began to take notice of quilts.

At about that time, Linda Reuther and Julie Silber opened a shop in California. It was called Mary Strickler's Quilts and catered to collectors as well as those wanting covers for their beds. In searching for quilts for the shop, they found some they could not bear to part with and so started a collection themselves. The shop has gone out of business, and some of the collection was auctioned at Sotheby's, but the women's names and influence remain an important link in the world of quilts-as-art. Julie Silber's mother, Merry, is also a well-known collector, specializing in Midwestern quilts.

By the end of the 1970s there were a number of collectors whose influence was felt and whose quilts were being shown in museums and galleries. David Pottinger and Darwin Bearley were authorities on and collectors of Amish quilts. In museum circles in New York the names of Cora Ginsberg, Cyril Nelson, and Robert Bishop were mentioned as authorities, while pieces from their collections became staples of quilt and folk art shows and were often seen in print.

Edwin Binney III and his daughter, Gail Binney Winslow, started collecting as a way of preserving the best of American quilts. They also had a great deal of fun, giving

RIGHT: **Freedom Star was designed and made by a traditional quiltmaker, Effie Rhodes Bell of Pender County, North Carolina, to commemorate the 1981 release of the hostages from Iran. The red-white-and-blue star design and the yellow ribbons in the center speak for themselves. The fifty-two blue print squares represent the number of hostages, and the white crosses the men killed in the rescue attempt. The Birds in Flight above the center are doves, and the church at the bottom represents the prayers of the nation. The outer border contains 444 blue squares for the number of days the men were held captive. The dates and the maker's name are embroidered on the quilt. 91 x 104″**

BELOW, RIGHT: **A pieced and tied comforter from the mid-nineteenth century, Maine. Copperplate and roller-printed fabrics were used for this warm and useful quilt. Private collection**

each other quilts as gifts, and eventually writing a book called *Homage to Amanda,* the name taken from the maker of the first quilt in their collection. Like many other collectors, they take pride in giving their collection, quilt by quilt, to museums. The New England Quilt Museum has been the recipient of a number of their treasures. Many other collectors are finding homes for their collections in museums that will take good care of them and give the public some access to them.

See also: Amish quilts, Museums

COMFORTERS

A standard item of bedding in America in the nineteenth century was the comforter, also called a "comfort" or a "comfortable." In some areas, especially Pennsylvania, it was also known by the North of England name "hap."

These serviceable coverings bore little resemblance to the fine Early American quilts, except that they, too, consisted of three layers. The top, often of wool and usually pieced with no design, was then tied through the batting to the backing with yarn or heavy string. The batting was often of wool also — sometimes, in very frugal households, an old blanket worn beyond any other usefulness.

See also: Haps, Tied quilts

COMMEMORATIVE QUILTS

Artists have often expressed their interest in world affairs and local events through their art, be it painting, sculpture, or quilts. Historically, women, having had fewer public outlets for their opinions than men, were therefore prolific in their artistic expression — the art often being quiltmaking. Wars, political campaigns, the temperance movement, and the Great Depression have all been the subjects of quilt designs.

In recent years horizons have been even broader. Sputnik set off a wider interest in what lies beyond our own global boundaries. Quilts have been designed to commemorate Halley's Comet and the exploration of space, as well as international

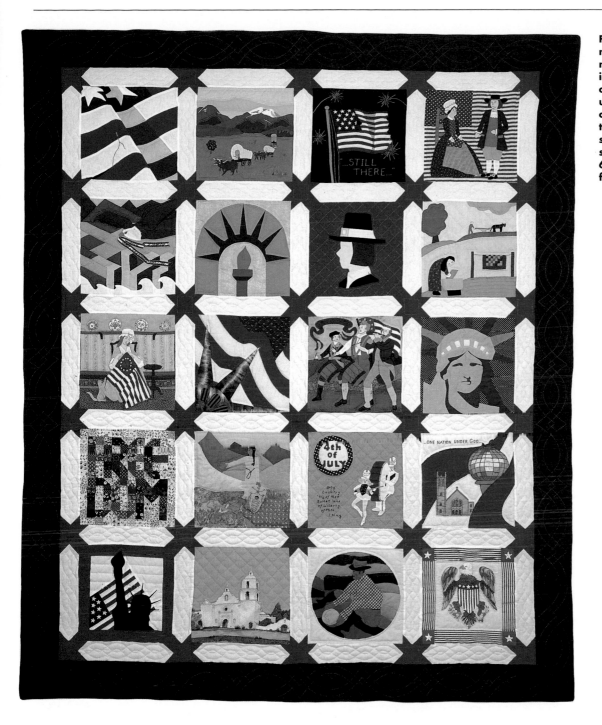

Fairfield Processing Corp., maker of quilt batting, also meets the needs of quilters in other ways. The American Heritage Quilt is made up of winning blocks from one of their annual contests. The company also sponsors an annual fashion show of quilted garments. 68 x 81″. Collection of Fairfield Processing Corp.

events such as the freeing of American hostages from Iran.

See also: Bicentennial quilts, Cause quilts, Centennial quilts, Patriotic quilts, Political quilts

COMPANIES

A great number of quilt-related companies have sprung up and flourished in the last hundred years. The manufacturers of batting, chiefly Mountain Mist and Fairfield Processing, also make other products, but their names are especially well-known for quilt batting. Textile companies have never been solely concerned with quilt fabrics, but

Conservation display, assembled by Kathleen McCrady for the 1988 Austin, Texas, quilt show

several have recently made great efforts to please that market in their over-the-counter lines, namely, Concord, Cranston, RJR, and Hoffman California.

The stories of companies started by one woman, employing any family member she could catch and working on the dining-room table are all true. Two such companies are Ladies' Art, which flourished from 1890 to about 1970, and *Quilter's Newsletter*, now one of the most important companies, publishing a monthly and a quarterly magazine; its sister company, Moon Over the Mountain, produces books. Bonnie Leman has been from its inception the head of this company — which has long since outgrown the dining-room table.

The Great Depression brought out the entrepreneurial abilities of quilters and those who recognized their special needs. Scotio Danner, a teacher from Kansas, set up Mrs. Danner's Patterns, now owned and run by Helen Ericson. Garrett Raterink of Grand Rapids, Michigan, turned his skills to

making quilting stencils under the name Needleart Guild. This company, now expanded, is still operated by the founder, his wife, and their daughter.
See also: Batting, Fabrics, Pattern companies, Stencils, Templates

CONSERVATION

As quilts are now considered collectibles, they must be cared for and preserved. When they were used as bedcovers and the family slept under them, the only concern was to keep them relatively clean. Constant washing, sunning, and airing led to the demise of many quilts. There were, however, others that were made for show, almost as works of art; these were preserved with great care and, in some cases, never washed.

It is often apparent that a cotton quilt has been well kept but was never washed — there is a glazed feeling to the surface that is lost when a quilt is immersed in water. To retain the original value of the quilt, it is advisable that it not be washed but sent to a

Glorious Lady Freedom by
Moneca Calvert was the
winner of the Great American Quilt Contest in 1986,
sponsored by the Museum
of American Folk Art, New
York, and the 3-M Corporation. The celebration of the
hundredth anniversary of
the Statue of Liberty occa-
sioned this outburst of
patriotism. 72 x 72″. The
Scotchguard Collection of
Contemporary Quilts

textile conservator for special cleaning. If
this choice seems too costly, there is only
one safe way of removing at least the surface
dirt. The quilt should be laid out on a flat,
clean surface and a section at a time covered
with a piece of fiberglass screening (not
wire) that has been carefully taped around
the rough edges. Any hand-held vacuum
with a clean small brush attachment may
then be used to draw the dust out through
the screening. The quilt is cleaned in sections, first on one side and then the other.

A good general rule is that cotton quilts

may be washed but should not be sent out
to the dry cleaner. Silk, velvet, or wool quilts
should never be washed but may be dry-
cleaned by a reputable cleaner. Good sources of advice on washing are quilting magazines and books and quilt-shop owners.

A continued controversy about storage
can make it difficult for the amateur collector to know how to care for quilts. There
are, however, some basic guidelines. The
dry, hot attic and damp basement are equally unsuitable storage places. The controversy concerns whether to roll or fold the

Small wall quilts made for the 1988 Invitational Challenge at Silver Dollar City's Fifth Annual Quilt Show, Branson, Missouri. Each piece was made from an original design by a well-known quilter using Springs Industries' Richmond Hill Fabric Collection by Marti Michell. Top, left: Red Star Rising by Chris Wolf Edmonds of Lawrence, Kansas; Top, right: Hilltop Houses by Flavin Glover of Auburn, Alabama; Bottom, left: Shades of the Old Carousel by Bettina Havig of Columbia, Missouri; Bottom, right: Christmas Kaleidoscope by Doreen Speckmann of Madison, Wisconsin

quilts. In either case it is wise to fold or roll acid-free tissue paper between the layers. If the quilt is to be folded, the paper should be crumpled into long rolls to prevent the folds in the quilt from making sharp creases. The quilts should be taken out, aired, and refolded along different lines every so often. Moth crystals should not be folded into the quilt but can be sprinkled at the backs of shelves to deter moths, silverfish, and mice from damaging the textiles.

If a quilt is to be hung as a work of art, it is wise to seek professional help with the method of hanging. It is absolutely necessary to keep it out of strong, direct light and away from windows and radiators. Rotating any textile art and giving each piece a dusting and a rest probably prolongs its life. *See also: Appraisals, Repair, Wall quilts, Washing*

CONTESTS

Contests are slightly different from judged or juried shows of other kinds in that they are often sponsored by a large organization, company, or commercial group. They are also usually juried, simply to keep the number of quilts manageable. There are frequently large money prizes but these are often "purchase" prizes, meaning that the winning quilts will not be returned to the maker. Companies and museums accumulate wonderful quilt collections this way and the quiltmakers profit nicely.

The prize quilts may or may not be shown at a special event, published in a book, or taken on tour. The winner of a local judged show takes her quilt home, uses it, enters it in further shows, and passes it on to her children or grandchildren. The winner of a contest basks in the glory of seeing her quilt publicized, accepts the money prize, but, if it is a purchase prize, says good-bye to that quilt.

See also: Judged shows, Juried shows, Prizewinning quilts, State fairs

COPPERPLATE PRINTING

Printing with blocks into which a design has been cut is one of the oldest ways of decorating textiles. In the mideighteenth century, copperplates of the kind used for printing on paper began to be used for more detailed and shaded designs on fabric. Larger plates made even more elaborate printing possible, and in 1752 an Irish invention for setting dyes brought the process up to a very sophisticated level. Other inventions contributed to more sophisticated printing presses on which lengths of cloth could be moved along, but full mechanization was never achieved. Copperplate printing came to an end about 1830, but not before the fashion was created for pictorial prints, notably the French scenic toile de Jouy.

See also: Block printing, Calico

CORDED QUILTING

Of all the varieties of raised and padded quilting, the most delicate and intricately beautiful is corded quilting. This process may have come originally from Italy and is sometimes called "trapunto." It appears on the fourteenth-century Sicilian quilt in the Victoria and Albert Museum and in much sixteenth- and seventeenth-century quilted bedding and clothing.

The technique requires two parallel lines of fine stitching holding the backing and the top fabric together. The space between the lines is only wide enough to allow a large blunt needle and heavy yarn or soft cord to be pulled through. The weave of the backing fabric must be loose enough to allow the needle and yarn to pass through easily. The result is a delicately raised composition on the surface fabric.

See also: Marseilles spreads, Stuffed work, Trapunto, Whole-cloth quilts

CORDING

There are two types of cord or cording used on quilts, most frequently in finishing the edges. "Cord" usually refers to the cotton cord laid inside fabric piping. This is then sewed in seams — as for the joining of blocks — or under the edge of binding, purely for decoration.

Silk — or, later, rayon — cording is also of two types. One is a round decorative cord with a lip, or flange, attached. It was most often used on the edge of silk or wool Victorian quilts, especially crazy quilts; the flange was sewn between the top and backing as with piping. The other type is also a round decorative cord, but without a lip or flange; it was attached by hand to the edge

RIGHT: The Kingston Heritage Quilters in Canada finish their work with the greatest care, often using a corded piping on the edge in place of binding and signing the piece with embroidery. (Detail)

BELOW: Ruth Fitch of Wichita, Kansas, collected print cotton fabrics from the late nineteenth century when Turkey red became popular. The Bow Tie pattern is from *Ladies Art,* 1898. The quilt was made in the 1980s, attesting to the lasting quality of cotton fabric

RIGHT: The Kingston Heritage Quilters in Canada finish their work with the greatest care, often using a corded piping on the edge in place of binding and signing the piece with embroidery. (Detail)

of Victorian quilts, after the top and backing had been sewn together.

See also: Piping

CORNER BLOCKS

When quilt blocks are set together with sashes or strips of contrasting fabric, the further addition of a corner block often adds interest to the design. A simple contrast of color may emphasize the juxtaposition of the sash and the corner block, or there may be some special design accent in the corner block that sets it apart. Common designs for corner blocks are nine-patch, four triangles, or a cross. The corners sometimes extend the rhythm of the main block design and sometimes stand alone as a sort of punctuation.

See also: Blocks, Sashes, Sets

COTTON

The staple fabric of quilting is — and has been for at least two centuries — cotton.

Early whole-cloth quilts and quilted petticoats were sometimes made of silk, while bed quilts were made of wool for warmth and utility into the nineteenth century. Any quilts that were made entirely of linen generally predate the importation of cotton from India in the seventeenth century, though in America homespun linen was still used as quilt backing well into the nineteenth century. Around 1800, the linsey-woolsey quilts also disappeared. From then until the middle of that century cotton was king.

In the middle of the last century some full-size bed quilts made of silk were pieced in traditional fashion, but the truly elegant album quilts of that time are of cotton, as were most household quilts. By 1880 there was a great movement to encourage women to produce more artistic needlework, including Victorian crazy quilts, and some women writing and lecturing at that time made disparaging remarks about cotton quilts. Judging by the number of fine late-nineteenth-century cotton quilts in existence, both pieced and appliqué, the remarks had little effect.

The recent quilting revival has had a profound effect on the manufacture of cotton print fabrics. Because quilters soon learned that all-cotton fabric is in most cases easier to work on and more effective after it is quilted than are cotton blends, the companies producing these fabrics have met the need with attractive lines of one hundred percent cotton fabrics. They have also produced more small prints and better lines of coordinated colors created especially for quilters. Though art quilts are made in a wide range of fabrics, most quilters today have returned to cotton as their first choice.
See also: Companies, Fabrics, Linen, Silk, Wool

COVERLETS

The term "coverlet" is used in at least two ways that concern quilters and collectors. Woven coverlets were made in America after 1820 on French jacquard looms. These pieces are double-woven and reversible, so that the handsome and often elaborate patterns appear in reverse colors on the two sides.

Another form of coverlet looks like a quilt top, usually appliqué, with a backing and no batting. These are often referred to as "summer coverlets," or "spreads." They were obviously used as decorative accessories and not for warmth.
See also: Spreads

CRADLE QUILTS

Tiny quilts have been made for many purposes such as doll beds, samples, or true miniatures for purely decorative purposes. Some are even cut down from larger, worn-out quilts. Some few are obviously made for the new baby and can be easily identified as

ABOVE: The appliqué Laurel Leaf blocks are set with dark sashes and borders with pieced corner blocks in both. The quilt was made in Pitt County, North Carolina, by Nancy Elizabeth Nelson in the late 1880s. 90 x 90″. Private collection

LEFT: A 1989 cradle quilt in the style of an earlier century. Helen Squire used a fine washable polyester crepe with a bias self-ruffle for this delicate whole-cloth quilt. 27 x 29″

cradle quilts. These are often made of soft, silky fabrics and are whole-cloth with no embellishment other than the quilting and

A counterpane or coverlet made in the Tree of Life quilt style but without batting. This piece with appliqué and embroidery — some in silk thread — was made in the midnineteenth century for Dr. Josiah Hasbrouck and his wife of Ulster County, New York. The figures of the man, woman, and two boys are said to be the Hasbrouck family. 99 x 80″. Courtesy of The Smithsonian Institution, Washington, D.C.

perhaps a ruffle or lace around the edge. They are smaller, daintier, and often lack the child-appeal of bright colors and lively designs found in crib quilts.

See also: Crib quilts, Miniature quilts

CRAZY QUILTS

It is tempting to believe that the first pieced quilts were crazy quilts, made up of random leftovers. It is hard to prove this theory because those very first quilts, perhaps from the seventeenth or eighteenth century, were made to be used and were worn out long before anyone was interested in documenting them.

In the late nineteenth century, the highly decorative and rather extravagant Victorian crazy quilt was born. It was made of silk and velvet — and sometimes wool — in rich dark colors and finished with heavy embroidery. Such quilts were not born of poverty.

By the first part of the twentieth century, the same free-form designs were being made in cottons, often embroidered as the earlier silk and velvets had been made. The simplification of tastes in clothing made the richer fabrics in shorter supply, and by the Depression of 1930, the crazy quilt was simply another candidate for cotton scrap.
See also: Scrap quilts and Victorian crazy quilts

CREPELINE

The finest and most nearly invisible silk fabric is crepeline. It comes in neutral colors and is the choice of conservators for covering and masking fabric that is beginning to disintegrate on the surface of a quilt. It is available through museum supply houses and sometimes in quilt shops.
See also: Conservation, Repair

CRIB QUILTS

The appeal of crib quilts is universal. The size, about forty-five by fifty-four inches, allows for a wide choice of styles and settings. Designs using six-inch or nine-inch blocks have long been popular. Many crib quilts have one large central composition that may depict a nursery rhyme, farmyard scene, or other childhood delight. Designs of this kind were very popular with the quilt-kit companies of the midtwentieth century. Fabric companies have made spe-

ABOVE: Crazy quilts were not always of silk and velvet but, like this one, ca. 1935, sometimes of familiar family cottons. Collection of Raymond Bosserman, Staunton, Virginia

LEFT: Boston Commons crib quilt with sawtooth edge. Hand-made and hand-finished by Mary Webb of Illinois, 1981. Collection of the author

A Dozen Plus, pieced and quilted by Ruth Him, 1983, from a design by Joyce Schlotzhauer. The curved two patch has made more fluid lines possible in piecing. 32 x 58". Courtesy of Joyce Schlotzhauer

cial panel prints, similar to cheater cloth, that can be put together with borders, batting, backing, and some quilting to make very attractive crib quilts.

See also: Blocks, Cheater cloth, Children's quilts, Cradle quilts, Juvenile quilts, Sets

CROSS-STITCHING

In the early twentieth century, all types of embroidery were popular for household linens and for quilts. The large needlework companies and design houses produced hot-iron transfers and entire kits with fabric already stamped. Cross-stitch reached the height of its popularity between 1920 and 1950. As far as can be deduced from existing samples of cross-stitch quilts, there were few if any original designs. The telltale blue design stamping is indelible and still shows under the edges of each stitch, no matter now carefully worked.

In recent years, some needleworkers have combined counted-thread cross-stitch on hardanger cloth (an even-weave fabric) with other fabrics to produce more original and interesting quilts. Kits for pastel floral designs on white are still available from the larger mail-order needlework houses.

See also: Embroidery

CURVED TWO-PATCH DESIGNS

Once in a while in quilting design a totally new and innovative method or pattern comes along. In 1982 Joyce Schlotzhauer's first book of Curved Two-Patch designs came on the market. She employed two simple shapes that, laid together, formed a small square. As these squares were joined, long flowing curves emerged, and shapes

heretofore impossible in pieced designs became possible. Florals far more graceful than those designed by Ann Orr and other earlier twentieth-century patternmakers are now available both to people who prefer piecing to appliqué and to people who piece on the sewing machine. There are now three books of patterns as well as instructions that enable the quilter to create her own designs.

See also: Pieced florals

DATING TEXTILES

One important part of appraising a quilt or any textile or antique is accurate dating. Sometimes there is no doubt of the date, because the maker embroidered it onto the quilt or wrote it somewhere on the back in indelible ink. Sometimes a quilt was so obviously designed for a special occasion — such as the 1933 Century of Progress Exposition in Chicago — that its date can be easily ascertained.

Fabrics that were printed for special occa-

sions, such as the Centennial or Bicentennial, were probably used within ten years of the time they were printed. A knowledgeable quilt expert or appraiser can recognize hundreds of fabrics by their design and color and can place them within ten or twenty years of their manufacture. One problem arises specific to quilts — the fabrics were not necessarily used at the time they were on the market. Often a quilt that was planned and partially cut out in 1920, for example, was put away, then rediscovered by a granddaughter in 1980 and finally finished. There have been at least two well-

known twentieth-century quiltmakers — Florence Peto in the first half and Anna Holland in this last quarter of the century — who planned and made quilts of antique fabrics that they collected. Without a date written or embroidered on the quilt, it is usually only possible to establish the time it was made within twenty or thirty years.
See also: Appraisal, Labels

DEPRESSION QUILTS

A term that is used by many quilt collectors and authorities but scorned by some is "Depression quilts," meaning those quilts

LEFT: **A medallion quilt made recently by Anna Holland of Waterford, Virginia, using chintz and other fabrics from the midnineteenth century. Though the fabrics are easily identifiable, the workmanship and elaborate quilting could be from any century. It might be difficult to date this quilt accurately, especially in another twenty years**

RIGHT: **This Ocean Waves with fan quilting is typical of country quilts in the Depression. It contains dress prints and feed-sack prints much used in the 1930-40s. The background is utility-grade muslin and the batting is very heavy. 68 x 72". Collection of the author**

Pieced Early American Wreath is one of the best-known of Ann Orr's floral designs. This one was made by Addie Libby of Jefferson, Oregon, late in her 96th year, ca. 1940. Private collection

were vivid and the range of hues in solid cottons rivaled the rainbow. Even the most traditional patterns sparkle with the tiny fragments of color and print in the scrap quilts of the 1930s.
See also: Feed sacks, Kit quilts

DESIGNERS

So many quilters design their own patterns that it is almost impossible to designate anyone as purely a quilt designer. There are, however, names that arise in any discussion of the great influences on quilting in America. Probably the first designer to be known by name and whose influence is still felt is Mary Evans Ford of Baltimore. Her nineteenth-century Baltimore album designs, especially the baskets, are familiar today to anyone concerned with quilts.

The twentieth century produced a number of designers whose creations are still in use. Marie Webster's patterns appeared early in the century in the *Ladies' Home Journal*, at about the same time as Ann Orr's in *Good Housekeeping*. Ruby Short McKim had her own studio and published a book, *101 Patchwork Designs*, which is still in print. These women were able artists and designers — Ruby McKim had attended Parson's School of Design and another well-known designer, Rose Kretsinger, taught at the Art Institute of Chicago. She made up the beautiful flowing appliqué tops that she designed, although she had them quilted by someone else, as did many expert needlewomen in that period.

The new wave of quilting that swept over the country after the Bicentennial has produced so many designers that it would be impossible to name them all. Small compa-

made in the economically bleak 1930s. There were, of course, quilts made in those years that have nothing to do with the hard times of the era, lovely appliqué gardens and even the most extravagant kit quilts. There are, however, an enormous number of scrap quilts, obviously created from odds and ends, including feed sacks, with which impoverished quilters had to make do.

The surprise qualities of true Depression quilts are the brilliance and variety of the fabrics. There are several reasons for this beside the fact that people in those days must have needed something to cheer them. There was a larger variety of prints available in cotton fabrics than ever before or since, probably because labor and manufacture were cheap. The colors used in textile dyes nies have sprung up, producing both original and traditional designs. Typical of these is One of a Kind Designs, owned and operated by Patricia Cox, who is a fine quilter, too.

There are also designers who go unsung, except as occasional prizewinners in large shows or contests. Such people are not interested in making commercial patterns but in working out their own original designs for their own satisfaction. The best way to see the achievements of such artists is to see the winners of any large contest in which originality is a major factor.

See also: Art quilts, Contests, Patterns

DESIGN SOURCES

Quilters take design ideas from everything that crosses their line of vision, Arabic tiles and farm animals being two very different subjects high on the list of favorites. Contests have inspired new floral designs, landscapes, and a wide spectrum of memories and geometric arrangements. Children's coloring books, with their simple, strong graphics, have always been a good source for appliqué designs. Even a postcard can inspire a quilter! The traditional School House pieced-block design has been reworked to resemble individual houses or villages, proving that even familiar quilts can serve as sources for new designs.

See also: Folk patterns, Indian influence, Japanese influence, Literary motifs, Tree motifs

DIAMONDS

Certain shapes are especially suited to repeating patterns — chief among them the diamond, both 45° and 60°. In quilts, both of these are frequently used in star forma-

tions. The great Star of Bethlehem and Broken Star compositions are all made up of 45° diamonds. The 60° diamond is more flexible and can be interchanged with hexagons, equilateral triangles, and parallelograms to form a great array of designs and many optical illusions. Not only were these shapes used in some of the first pieced quilts

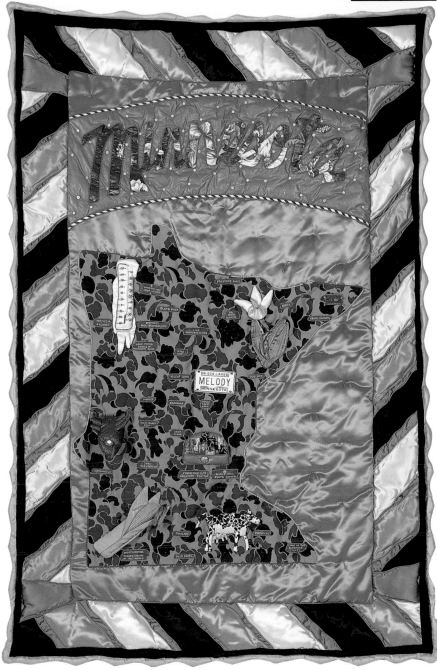

Minnesota Postcard quilt, 1979, by Teresa Nomura. The right side of the quilt has soft-sculpture corn, lady slippers, fish, etc. The reverse side is an exact replica of a postcard with a long message in blue textile ink. 62 x 43″. Collection of the Minnesota Historical Society, St. Paul, Minnesota

A 60° diamond is one of the favorite shapes for quilt design. It is usually seen in a Six-Point Star, but this silk Quaker quilt, made in 1852 by Sarah Taylor Middleton Rogers of Crosswicks, New Jersey, has double that number. 103 x 103". Collection of the American Museum in Britain, Claverton Manor, Bath, England. Gift of Mary Middleton Rogers, granddaughter of the maker

but they can be seen as well in Near-Eastern tiles from many centuries earlier.
See also: Hexagons, Star designs

DISCHARGE PRINTING

Printers and dyers of fabric the world over have looked for ways to make colors fast and designs clear. This search, along with a multiplicity of inventions, gained momentum in the early nineteenth century. Among the solutions to the problem is discharge printing, still employed today in some form.

The method is almost exactly the opposite of resist dying. The fabric is first dyed in a solid color — frequently indigo, as immersion is the only way to apply that dye to fabric — producing an even and sometimes more color-fast background. The design is then printed in acid and the fabric processed so that the color is lifted from the printed areas. The result is a white or light design on a dark background.
See also: Block printing, Copperplate printing, Dyes, Resist-dye blue prints

The Star of Bethlehem with eight points is made up of 45° diamonds. This quilt was made by Henrietta Johnson Wilson of Louisville, Kentucky, in 1850. Collection of the Henry Ford Museum and Greenfield Village, Dearborn, Michigan

DOCUMENTATION

As quilts have become an increasingly important part of textile collections, it has become desirable to document them as accurately as possible. Lucky the museum or collector who finds a quilt with names and dates and other pertinent information either boldly worked into the design of the quilt or carefully inked or embroidered on either front or back. The next best record is the family history of the maker, written down and kept with the quilt.

In recent years there have been state quilt searches and projects whose sole purpose has been to document the quilts that have been cared for by and are often still in the families of the makers' descendants. Systems of documentation have been perfected and files maintained for future reference. As knowledge accumulates, it becomes easier to pinpoint the dates and locales of many quilts and to connect the missing links in family — and especially women's — history. Local museums are often ready to help document quilts.

See also: Appraisals, Dating textiles, Labels, State quilt projects

DOLL QUILTS

The idea of a doll quilt is so appealing that many of these small gems have probably been made for the sheer joy of making them, as often as for a child or a doll bed. Some small pieces that pass for doll quilts are really segments cut from worn-out quilts. At this time, when miniature quilts are enjoying unprecedented popularity, it is increasingly hard to tell a real doll quilt — one made for the purpose — from miniatures created especially to hang on a wall. *See also: Miniature quilts*

DYES

As printed cloth is a vital element of quilts, so are dyes essential to cloth. The decoration of textiles has been important to civilized peoples for centuries; dyes have been traded — even used as currency — throughout the world for five thousand years or more. One of the best-known examples of the wealth acquired from dying fabric is that of the Phoenicians, whose true purple dye, from a shellfish of the genus *Purpura*, was known as Tyrian purple, reserved for royalty. The Phoenicians plied their trade throughout the known world long before the birth of Christ.

Different plants were used in different parts of the world to make dyes for cloth and leather. The secrets were often closely guarded and the processes quite varied, depending on the mordants used and the combinations of plant or animal products that created shading and permanence. We have records of early knowledge of madder, an herb of the genus *Rubia*, used for red; saffron, from the orange stigmas of a crocus, for yellow; and woad, a mustard plant whose leaves made a blue dye. Eventually indigo, from the plant of the same name, took the place of woad. Most of the Early American blue fabrics seen in quilts are indigo, either resist-dyed or discharge-printed. Indigo is a difficult medium to apply, because it cannot be block- or plate-printed but must be immersed, then undergo several subsequent processes. It was also used in combination with yellow dyes to create green.

The nineteenth century saw the discovery of dyes other than the natural ones used in previous centuries. From the time the first permanent green dye was devised in 1810 until the discovery of a really workable blue aniline dye in 1880, the development of synthetic dyes became increasingly important to the fledgling textile industry.

In spite of the progress in mass-produced textiles, it is still possible to find American quilts containing home-dyed fabrics created well into the twentieth century. Many women lived with little access to stores and were familiar with dyes made from common garden plants and trees — marigold, walnut, and so forth. Frugality demanded that such material as white flour sacks be used, at least for the backs of quilts — but the demands of frugality did not go so far as to prohibit making them more attractive with the addition of homemade color.

See also: Block printing, Copperplate printing, Discharge printing, Fugitive color

EDGING

Many techniques are used to finish the edges of quilts, from the purely practical to the elaborately decorative. The most common edge is a simple binding. This may be a thin strip of cloth, either straight-grain or bias, or it may be self-binding, formed by bringing the edge of the backing over the edge of the top and batting. With any of these a fine corded piping may be a decorative detail just under the edge of the binding.

Two finishes seen on early quilts are now rarely, if ever, used. For the first, the quilter simply turned in both top and backing and slip-stitched the two together without adding any decoration. The second is a narrow woven tape, made on a tiny and now obsolete tape loom. In the early nineteenth century many quilters had such looms and wove their own tape.

Sawtooth and prairie point edges both

give the effect of sharp points all around the quilt. Both were popular in the midnineteenth century and are still widely used, especially among traditional quilters.

In the late Victorian era elaborate edgings were used, especially on silk and velvet quilts. It was a time of cords and tassels, ruffles, and heavy lace.
See also: Binding, Cording, Piping, Ruffles, Self-binding

EMBROIDERY

A great array of embroidery has adorned quilts, either alone or with other techniques. The details on appliqué are usually worked in outline or chain stitch and French knots. In *broderie perse*, the edges of the appliqué itself are frequently laid down with buttonhole or herringbone stitch. Many signature and fund-raising quilts have minimal patterns enhanced by hundreds of embroidered names. The main point of Victorian crazy quilts at the height of their popularity was to demonstrate the number of inventive embroidery stitches that could be used in sewing down the patches.

The first third of the twentieth century, until about 1935, saw a wave of red-on-white embroidered quilts, often with matching pillowcases. These were usually worked in blocks with the simplest of embroidery stitches. The patterns were sold in stores and through magazines, either as hot-iron transfers or as pieces of muslin already stamped. They were so simple that they were considered ideal learning pieces for children and were offered to young quilters through *Child Life* magazine.

Cross-stitch kit quilts have also been popular in this century. Such companies as Lee Wards and Herrschner's still carry a line of these designs in their catalogues.
See also: Cross-stitching, Victorian crazy quilts

ENGLISH PIECING

Designs made up of small geometric pieces — hexagons and diamonds, for example — are difficult to seam together evenly. The English have traditionally made these as one-patch designs, often in silk, chintz, and other such hard-to-handle fabrics. They

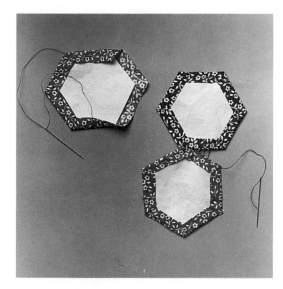

ABOVE, LEFT: English piecing is a method of stabilizing odd shapes with a paper backing while they are being joined together

ABOVE, RIGHT: A back view of an unfinished section of English piecing from the Haynes family, ca. 1850. Collection of the D.A.R. Museum, Washington, D.C. 85.7

BELOW: Typical pieced medallion-style English quilt from the late eighteenth century. Such quilts often seem to be display pieces for elegant block- and plate-printed cottons rather than having the kind of geometric organization of American pieced quilts. 94 x 91". The Metropolitan Museum of Art, New York. Rogers Fund and Spring Mills, Inc. Gift, 1975, 1975.2

invented a method of basting each piece over a paper template and whipping the edges together while the paper holds the fabric flat. When the joining is completed, the paper is removed and the quilt finished in the usual manner. This method of joining is still called "English piecing" and continues to be used on some difficult patterns and delicate fabrics.

A number of English-pieced tops have been found in an unfinished state. Interestingly, the paper templates were made of writing or other papers that gave researchers clues to the circumstances of the person who started the quilt or the time in which it was made.

See also: Diamonds, Hexagons, One-patch designs

ENGLISH QUILTS

The story of quilts and quilted clothing goes back very far in English history. Writings from as early as the fifteenth century refer to "twylts" — the word later became "quylt" and then "quilt." Few remnants of early quilts remain but there are many written references to petticoats and bed coverings made of various fabrics with wadding of wool, and later of cotton. The early pieces were what we now call whole-cloth quilts, two layers of fabric with batting between and stitched in attractive patterns.

There was an industry centered around quilting that included both the making of quilts and clothing and the marking of designs for other people to work. Men as well as women were employed as quilters.

After chintz arrived from India, throughout the eighteenth century and into the nineteenth, pieced quilts and unquilted pieced coverlets became popular. The two types of design that are seen most often from the nineteenth century in England are the beautifully quilted strippy quilts, which seem to be forerunners of the Amish bars, and medallion quilts, with a strong central image framed by borders. They crossed the ocean to the United States, where they remain popular.

Another pieced design that has been used in England for at least two hundred years is the Hexagon Mosaic, forerunner of the American Grandmother's Flower Garden. The large stars made of 45° diamonds were also worked on both sides of the Atlantic.

The most tasteful chintz appliqué quilts were made in England as well as among the English in America in the late eighteenth and early nineteenth centuries. It is probable that people able to afford a gracious way of life were in close correspondence with relatives across the ocean, and may actually have visited one another. The fabrics and the ideas would have traveled also.

See also: Chintz, Hexagons, Marking, Medallion quilts, Mosaics, Strippy quilts

FABRICS

Traditionally, quilts have been made of almost any fabric that has ever been woven: cotton, linen, silk, and wool. Early European quilts were not made of cotton because it was a rarity until the cloth was imported in quantity from India in the seventeenth century. The earliest American quilts were made of wool, though some were of linen, both probably homespun. Cotton became the fabric of choice at the end of the eighteenth century.

The invention of workable roller presses in the late eighteenth century made small repeat prints an affordable reality for many women. The production and processing of cotton in America added great excitement and variety to the quilts in the first half of the nineteenth century. Silk-pieced full-size bed quilts were popular in the affluent time just prior to the Civil War, and wool quilts almost disappeared.

After the Civil War the greater range of fabrics used in quilts may have been a by-product of the necessary frugality in many parts of the country. The Log Cabin pattern was very popular and was often worked in wools or silks or a combination of materials — obviously leftover scraps from the family dressmaking. The next trend was the Victorian crazy quilt, with its helter-skelter mixture of silks, velvets, occasional wools, and even bits of lace and embroidery cut from worn garments.

In the twentieth century cotton has been the predominant fabric in quilting. With mechanization, synthetic dyes, and better distribution, wonderful smooth-textured calicoes and muslins have been the basics of quiltmaking. Synthetic fabrics have not become widely popular, and most quiltmakers have returned to one hundred-percent cotton, rather than blends.

See also: Calico, Muslin, Roller printing, Victorian crazy quilts

FASHION

Clothing has been quilted almost as long as fabric has been layered and stitched together. In recent years it has been more than just pretty and utilitarian — it has moved into high fashion as well as the mainstream.

Sport jackets and coats of quilted synthetic fabric with goose-down filler have appeared on racks from L. L. Bean to Saks Fifth Avenue. Fashion designers, both American and European, have quilted elegant fabrics, especially for evening wear.

The Fairfield Fashion Show has become an important annual event for quilters and craftspeople. The top quilt designers are invited to create garments to be shown at a number of large quilt shows during the

Virginia Avery creates fashions for herself and for Fairfield's annual fashion show. This coat with quilted lining and dress with quilted jewelry is called There'll Be a Hot Time in the Old Town Tonight. Collection of the Fairfield Processing Corp.

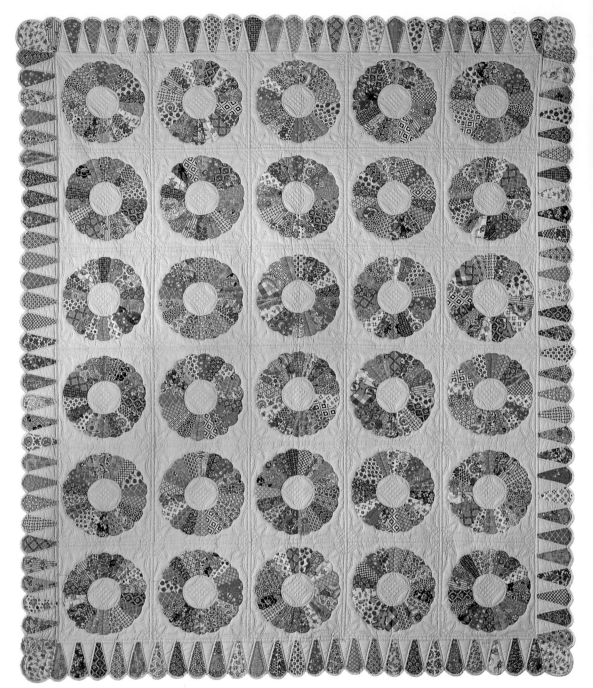

Dresden Plate design with Ice Cream Cone border, pieced entirely of feed-sack fabrics by Shirley Miller, ca. 1980, and quilted by the Pioneer Quilters of Oregon. The last feed sacks were printed in the early 1950s. These were collected for the purpose of making this typical Depression quilt as a tribute to an earlier generation. 87 x 103″. Private collection

year — not only in the United States but internationally. As is the case with high-fashion shows in Paris and Milan, the garments are often extreme but serve to spark ideas for more wearable garments for the general public.

See also: Clothing, Wearable art

FEED SACKS

For over a hundred years in America many staples of farm life have come packed in plain white cotton bags. Not only feed for the livestock but sugar, flour, and other products were packaged in this way. The larger bags, those that held chicken feed, for example, provided about a yard and a quarter of thirty-five-inch or forty-five-inch fabric. Most of these feed sacks had a bold print to identify the product. If a farm woman used these for quilt backing, she took advantage of the whole piece of cloth and did not cut away the printing. If she used the piece for a quilt top, usually in blocks, she was more apt to get rid of the advertising.

Around the time of the Great Depression, some of the feed companies were quick to see the advantage of having the sacks printed in the cheerful floral, geometric, and juvenile prints so popular in yard goods. A supplier to one such company was Bemis Bags in Minnesota. These prints came as a gift to the quilters in the periods before, during, and after World War II, about twenty years in all. No record has been kept of the number of available prints, but the multiplicity of scrap quilts of the time is amazing.

See also: Backings, Depression quilts

FIBERS

Until the advent of synthetic fibers such as nylon and polyester, all fibers from which fabric was woven were vegetable or animal. With the exception of silk, which arrived in the Western world from the Orient at about the time of the Crusades, all of the natural fibers known and used today — cotton, linen, and wool — were in use in Egypt in the time of the Pharaohs. Except for linen, the other natural fibers are still used in quilts and thought by most quilters to be superior to synthetics.

See also: Cotton, Linen, Silk, Wool

FLAG QUILTS

Flags are an obvious source of design for quilters — colorful, straight-line design,

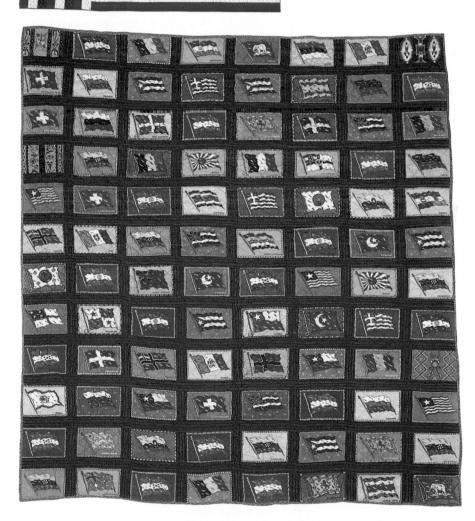

Hawaiian Flag quilt, made 1898 as a wedding gift for Rosina Georgetta Kalanikauwe-kiulani Ayers when she married Dr. Robert Henry Dinegar. At the time of the annexation of Hawaii by the United States, these quilts with the Hawaiian flag and royal coat-of-arms became very popular. 93 x 90″. Courtesy of The Smithsonian Institution, Gift of Adelaide Dinegar/McDonough

Flannel flags were early twentieth-century tobacco premiums and were frequently collected for quilts. This one was made by Pearlie Buck Spain of Pitt County, North Carolina, ca. 1920. 72 x 78″. Collection of Ruth Haslip Roberson

patriotic, and exciting. The fact that they
may not be appropriate for covering beds is
irrelevant, for they were made for entirely
different reasons — to celebrate the Centennial or Bicentennial, or the entrance of
the quiltmaker's state into the Union.

Probably the best-known flag quilts are
those from Hawaii, made at the turn of the
century after the abdication of the Hawaiian
queen. They display both the Hawaiian and
American flags and are certainly made for
show rather than use on a bed.

In wartime, flag quilts have been especially popular. Just before and during World
War I, the cigarette companies issued premiums of little cotton flannel flags of all
nations that were collected by quilters. The
fabric was one of the cheapest available at
the time, but the printing must have been
remarkably good, because it has stood up
well to the test of time and wear. One such
quilt in the collection of Joyce Aufderheide
was probably made during World War I,
because all of the German flags have been
used upside down. The name of each country is clearly printed beside the flag — in
the case of the Chilean flag, it is often
identified as "Chili."
See also: Cigarette premiums, Hawaiian quilts

FLORAL MOTIFS

Flowers and leaves, realistically portrayed or
stylized, are found in the earliest textile
designs. They were woven, printed, painted,
and embroidered in the oldest existing
remnants of decorated cloth.

Quilters have used floral designs in all
techniques. The early cutout chintz, or
broderie perse appliqué, is almost exclusively
floral. As soon as quilters began to make

pieced patterns representing anything
beside stars and baskets, they turned to
tulips and a sort of peony or lily made from
an eight-pointed star, which were the basic
pieced flowers. Appliqué continues to be
based in large part on flowers, especially
roses. All-white or whole-cloth quilts and
trapunto or other padded designs often
include flowers.

Until recently there have been a limited
number of pieced floral designs because it
was difficult to make them look graceful.
The curved two-patch system, designed by
Joyce Schlotzhauer, has made a much wider
variety possible. Probably the most popular
appliqué floral patterns are a variety of Rose
of Sharon designs and the wonderfully
simple tulips.
*See also: Appliqué, Curved two-patch designs,
Pieced florals*

FOLK-ART QUILTS

As Americans moved westward, women
used the medium of the quilt to make pictures of the world around them or the world
they left behind. There are farm scenes,

A true folk art pictorial quilt, designed and made by Sarah Ann Gorgis of Pennsylvania in 1853. One of the few artistic areas open to women in the nineteenth century was needlework. Wildly original quilt designs often portrayed parts of their everyday lives. 96 x 98″. Collection of the Museum of American Folk Art, New York

flags, houses, and the memorabilia of a lifetime. These quilts are called story quilts or folk-art quilts, but they are originals, each one a statement about a particular woman's world at a special time.

See also: Story quilts

FOLK PATTERNS

Some quilt-block patterns seem to have evolved from simple shapes and simple ideas, rather than to have been designed. They have eventually been incorporated into many commercial pattern lines and have become more sophisticated with the years, but they are still open to much

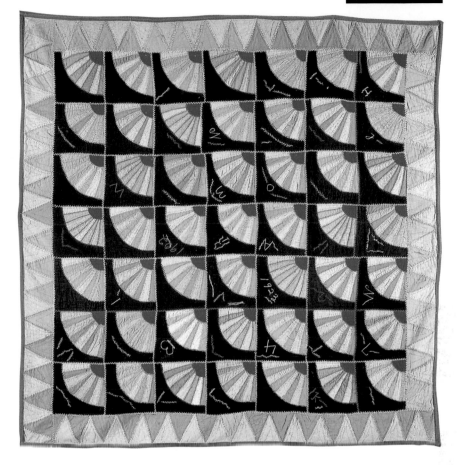

artistic changing and tampering.

The Fan design is a simple shape made with a compass or a pencil and a string. Creating Birds in Flight is a matter of cutting up one corner of the block into triangles. Right-angle triangles are natural extensions of a square and therefore appear again in Wild Goose Chase and many other folk patterns. The old English strippy quilts were the origin of Wild Goose Chase and many other American quilts that could be made quickly and attractively and put on the bed. The School House is probably the most sophisticated of the folk patterns, the kind of wonderful building that can be converted to look like a church, a home, or whatever the quilter needs to tell her story.

See also: Patterns

FOUNDATION PIECING

In the latter part of the nineteenth century, a technique called "foundation piecing" became very popular. Most innovations are born to meet some new and specific need, and it is highly possible that the impetus for this technique was the availability of silk in larger quantities at a much lower price than

before. A strong, thin muslin foundation made silk pieced work more durable. Patterns that were especially suited to this technique were those made up of same-size strips, such as Log Cabin and Pineapple, but the random Victorian crazy quilts were also made on muslin foundations.

See also: Log Cabin, Paper piecing, Pineapples, Press piecing, Strip piecing, Victorian crazy quilts

FOUR-PATCH DESIGNS

One very simple pieced unit is the four-patch. Two dark and two light squares are set together to make another, larger square. When these are pieced together, they will form interesting diagonal patterns. Children have traditionally been taught to piece

LEFT: Paper patterns, some from dated newspapers, for the Bird of Paradise quilt. Collection of the Museum of American Folk Art, New York

RIGHT: Fans are traditional folk patterns, needing no real paper template, and are simple to draft with a string, pin, and ruler. The results vary greatly. This one from Minnesota, made in 1922, included pieces of army blanket. 70 x 80". Collection of the Museum of American Folk Art, New York. Gift of Margaret Cavigga

FOLLOWING PAGE: A popular Amish arrangement of Fans has the blocks set back-to-back to create a wavy diagonal line. This one from Indiana, marked with the initials P.M., was made in 1931. 83 x 73". Collection of the Museum of American Folk Art, New York. Gift of David Pottinger

on some version of the four-patch.

The squares are often subdivided to form sixteen smaller squares in each block. By dividing some of the four-patch squares diagonally into triangles, a whole array of other blocks can be formed, such as Windmill Blades, Crosses and Losses, and Broken Dishes. *See also: Nine-patch designs, One-patch designs, Patterns*

FOUR-POSTER-BED QUILTS

There are many quilts, usually quite elegant ones, from the late eighteenth and early nineteenth centuries that have an odd shape with two corners cut away. As soon as one of these is put on a four-poster bed, the ingenuity of the design becomes evident. No rectangular quilt can ever be arranged so well around the lower posts!

FRAMES

Probably the most popular and nostalgic image associated with quilts is that of

women seated around a large frame — a quilting bee. Frames have changed somewhat to conform to the requirements of space and mobility, but the large rectangular standing frame has never disappeared. There are two reasons for this: there is no better way to stretch a quilt smoothly to achieve perfect final results, and it is still the only way for more than one person to work at quilting.

The ratchet frame is a large, standing, fairly permanent piece of furniture with long poles between the two ends. The poles can be shifted to accommodate wider or narrower quilts, and the tension on the quilt can be adjusted by turning the poles; the ratchets hold each turn firmly. This type of

ABOVE, LEFT: **A four-patch doll-bed quilt made of antique fabrics by Gwen Marston, 1984. 13 x 16". Collection of the author**

Above, right: **Full Blown Poppy, made by Lucy Howland Bassett Thatcher of Lee, Massachusetts, ca. 1860. The cutout corners are accommodations for a four-poster bed. The pieced flower is similar to a pattern known as Caesar's Crown — all the leaves, vines, and buds are appliqué. The sawtooth edge finish is made of folded tape. 98 x 93". Collection of the D.A.R. Museum, Washington, D.C. 3825**

TOP: In early log cabins and other small pioneer homes the "four stout sticks" that served as a quilting frame were often suspended from the ceiling when not in use. Collection of the Saline County Museum, Illinois, the interior of the Aydelott House, a permanent exhibit in the museum

MIDDLE: A typical nineteenth-century ratchet quilt frame. The round metal piece, called a sawblade ratchet, serves to prevent the tightened rollers from slipping. Collection of Belle Grove Plantation, Middletown, Virginia. The quilt was made in the late nineteenth century by the Glaize sisters of Frederick County, Virginia. Private collection

BOTTOM: A modern commercial version of a standard wooden quilting frame and a standing quilting hoop

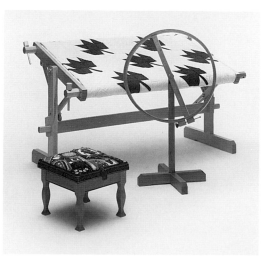

frame is considered by many quilters to be ideal for an evenly stretched quilt.

The simplest large frame is made of "four stout sticks," as Ruth Finley called them in her book, *Old Patchwork Quilts and the Women Who Made Them.* These poles, usually two-by-fours, can be of any length that will accommodate the quilt and are held firmly together at the corners with C-clamps. They are then set up with a straight chair or other support under each corner. Ladder-backed chairs are ideal, as the height of the frame can be changed by using any one of the crosspieces in the back of the chair as the support. Sometimes a simple stand is built for each corner to support the frame at the same height every time it is set up. Many pioneer homes and mountain cabins were too small to accommodate a frame set up for long periods of time, so the frame just described was hung on pulleys from the ceiling. When it was taken up, the free edge was hooked in place with simple screen-door hooks.

Quilters today have resorted to many other ways of holding a quilt taut during the quilting process. There are round standing frames and large lap hoops, in which the quilt must be moved so that each area is held taut as it is being quilted. Some people quilt without a frame, depending only on firm basting to hold the fabric smooth. Many professionals, however, believe that only one of the large frames can produce professional results.
See also: Hoops, Quilting

FREEDOM QUILTS

Mothers and friends have traditionally made bridal quilts for young women or wedding quilts for couples. Friendship quilts have been made for many people, but predominantly by women for women. When young men grow up and leave home mothers and sisters want to honor them, too, and so the freedom quilts came into being, probably in the nineteenth century. Some were made by a mother or sister alone and some by a group, in the manner of a friendship quilt.

Mixed feelings must have gone into these quilts, especially at a time when so many young men were going west, into the great unknown. Of course each family hoped that their son would be the one who made good, found gold, or homesteaded the right piece of land, but it helped a little to know that the young man took with him the warm cover made with such love and care. A few seem to have been made by a group of young women who must have felt some regret that one more prospective bridegroom was removed from their midst. Perhaps related to the freedom quilts was the legend concerning an early pattern called Wandering Foot. Any person sleeping under a quilt of this pattern would, it was said, leave home early and become a wanderer.

See also: Album quilts, Friendship quilts, Patterns

FRIENDSHIP QUILTS

In the decades just before the Civil War, distances were vast — when friends moved away, they might never be seen again. One way of being remembered for a long time was by making a friendship quilt. Groups of people, friends and family, worked on such a quilt, usually in blocks to allow more participation. Each block was signed in ink or with a small inked stamp, or the maker's

name might be embroidered. The quilt then traveled west or to some new home with the owner, to whom it gave a nostalgic sense of love and security.

A modern variation on the friendship quilt is a quilt made for the member of a guild. Usually a drawing is held by those members of the group who have not yet been presented with a quilt. The winner may get to choose her theme or her fabrics. Sometimes the winner or recipient is selected by birthday or length of time in the group. The blocks may be signed, or the signatures may be on the back of the quilt or on a special label.

See also: Album quilts, Autograph quilts, Group quilts, Signature quilts

Friendship quilt from the Warner family of Bucks County, Pennsylvania, with sixty-four blocks and forty-seven signatures. The inscription in the center wreath reads, "Twined for my daughter Rebecca Warner, Yardleyville, 1857." Most of the blocks are appliqué and some are chintz cutouts in the *broderie perse* style. 88 x 87". Collection of the Mercer Museum, Doylestown, Pennsylvania. 86.1601

This Bird Tree appliqué from 1880-85 seems as fresh and unworn as the day it was made. The difference is that the soft brown was once green — a fugitive color. 62 x 76". Collection of America Hurrah, New York City

FUGITIVE COLOR

When experts such as collectors and appraisers talk about quilts they frequently mention "fugitive color" or "fugitive dye." The simple definition is a color that fades or disappears or turns to another shade. A common example is the slightly metallic tan that was once green. The fabric under the edge of appliqué or at an inside seam that has not been exposed to light can often give a clue to the original color.

The problem of fading is common to both natural and synthetic dyes. It probably has more to do with the total process, such as the mordants used to set the dye and the length of time and number of steps, than with the actual dye. For example, to achieve the much-prized Turkey red dye, which became popular in the early nineteenth century and almost disappeared in World War I, required over twenty steps. Naturally this added greatly to the cost.

Some dyes in the latter half of the nineteenth century were not just fugitive, they were lethal! Intense fabric deterioration, especially in dark colors and silk, is common in fabrics of this period. Small prints in which a dark color was used on red now often appear only as a series of small holes in the background color.

See also: Dating textiles, Dyes

FUND-RAISER QUILTS

The community spirit of quilters is evident in many ways. Not only have they made quilts for the needy and for raffles and sales, but the fund-raising signature quilt has helped to lay the foundation for many churches and furthered many public causes.

The design of a fund-raiser quilt is usually very simple, allowing many people of varied skills to work on it. Sunflower and Dresden Plate patterns continue to be popular, because the small strips that make up the main block design can be handed out like raffle tickets. The right to sign one's name is sold for a small sum, and an indelible pen is usually provided. At its finest and most elaborate, the fund-raiser is enhanced by the fine embroidery of some member of the participating group. Traditionally, the inked signatures were made more permanent and more decorative by being worked over in fine stitchery.

Fund-raisers are automatically records of

a time and place and the people who lived there. They are extremely useful to anyone doing research on the history of a church, for example, or a small town.

See also: Autograph quilts, Signature quilts

A fund-raising quilt in a Log Cabin style, 1913, First United Methodist Church of Monongah, West Virginia. Here is a fine example of a signed and dated quilt with all the writing embroidered lastingly on the firm wool fabrics, mostly of men's suitings. 68 x 68". Collection of the West Virginia Department of Culture and History, Charleston, West Virginia

The light and airy Garden Maze setting and the subject matter of blocks like the Loving Couple suggest that this quilt, from the Demarest family of Hackensack, New Jersey, was a bride's quilt. It is signed in several places and dated 1876. 82 x 90". Collection of the Newark Museum, Newark, New Jersey. 48.1

GARDEN MAZE

A quilt pattern that appeared in the early nineteenth century, the Garden Maze, later reappeared as a setting for blocks of other patterns. The three narrow strips that form the rectangular part of the pattern are pieced. The crosspieces in the square are sometimes pieced but often appliqué. The center square can be opened up into a block of any size to accommodate any type of block pattern — the original pattern then becomes a setting of sashes and corner blocks.

See also: Corner blocks, Sashes, Sets

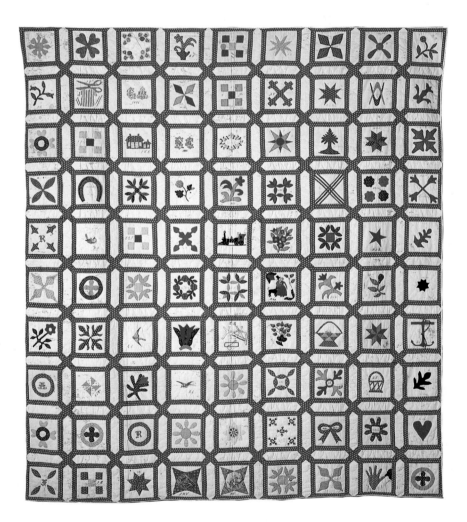

GENEALOGICAL QUILTS

Women have always used needles and fabric to express their feelings and to record history and memories. It is natural that family history would be high on the list of subjects for the quilt-as-permanent-record. The diversity of such family-tree or genealogical quilts is as broad as the backgrounds of the makers. They range from small wall hangings, made as wedding gifts, to the elaborate chintz medallions of the early nineteenth century. One design in recent years is a crossword puzzle with large letters in squares spelling out the names of family members. Quite a few are true family trees: large, sprawling trees sport names embroidered in place. Even family faces have been depicted in photographic printing on cloth.

See also: Memory quilts

GEOMETRY

There is a natural, often intricate, geometry to much quilt design. Even the seemingly simple process of dividing the entire surface of a quilt into blocks, sashes, and borders to achieve the correct size for a specific bed requires careful calculating. Different widths of sashes and the placement of the blocks can make the same block design vary greatly in appearance from one maker to the next.

The basic shapes most used by quilters are squares, hexagons (with their many variables), octagons, and triangles. The changing and interlocking of one or more of these shapes can produce beautiful tile effects, representational designs like stars and trees, and delightful abstractions of light and dark.

Hundreds, if not thousands, of block designs can be grouped into categories such as four-patch, nine-patch, and so on. Some

blocks are divided into five squares along each side, making a total of twenty-five squares and unlimited design possibilities. Some knowledge of geometry may be helpful in designing or creating patterns for known designs, but a ruler and a triangle or T-square plus the most basic arithmetic have made it possible for women to produce an immense variety of quilt blocks.

See also: Blocks, Four-patch designs, Hexagons, Nine-patch designs, Octagons, One-patch designs, Patterns, Squares, Triangles

GLAZED FABRICS

Homespun woolens were used for quilts and coverlets in eighteenth-century America. As houses became more grand, people wished to furnish them with more elegant fabrics. Some fabrics, such as silk, have a natural sheen, but it has always been a challenge to the manufacturers of cottons and wools to add a glaze to their finish. Chintz was one of the first cotton fabrics with a high glaze. Wool was glazed by a heat process that made a smooth and attractive finish. One name for this fabric, as it appears today in museum quilts, is "calimanco."

The glazing methods have undergone great changes, from the use of wax and a smooth stone to today's rapid machines.
See also: Calimanco, Chintz, Wool

GODEY'S LADY'S BOOK

From 1830 to 1898 no woman interested in style or needlework would have been without the magazine *Godey's Lady's Book.* The source of designs, patterns, and information, *Godey's* was the last word in fashion — for the home as well as the woman. There has probably never been another women's magazine as influential.

Quilts were mentioned and shown in *Godey's,* but few designs originated in its pages. During part of the publication's life, Victorian crazy quilts were popular, and information and embroidery designs for them appeared often. Silk and velvet were the quilting fabrics highly recommended for the fashion-conscious readers of *Godey's. See also: Victorian crazy quilts*

GRANDMOTHER'S FLOWER GARDEN

Hexagon designs are among the oldest of all geometrics, dating from the dawn of civilization. English quilts from before 1800 employed them in great variety, including a floral pattern eventually known as Grandmother's Flower Garden. Any hexagonal, or honeycomb, piecing was more easily handled with the English piecing method and so became associated with English quilting rather than with American.

In the twentieth century, when pattern companies and newspaper patterns for quilts became popular, Grandmother's Flower Garden appeared in every line of patterns. The pieces were often larger than those used in English piecing, and the method recommended for joining them was often the same running stitch used for any other pieced pattern. There was hardly a needlewoman alive in the 1920s and 1930s who did not make at least one Grandmother's Flower Garden, an ideal design for scrap. The large majority were made with a white background, and each "petal" was carefully cut to show off some specific section of each print. Some patterns had a garden walk of diamonds and triangles, usually in solid green, carefully fitted around each flower motif.

See also: English piecing, Geometry, Hexagons, Mosaics

GROUP QUILTS

A most enjoyable aspect of the art of quilting is that two or more can play. One of the most enduring — and endearing — images of early American life is the quilting bee. Not only did many hands lighten the load, but hardworking women who lived otherwise fairly solitary lives were able to justify a day's outing with a group of friends.

Quilts have been not only finished by groups working at frames but they have also been made, block by block, by several friends or members of an organization. The

friendship, album, and presentation quilts, so popular in the second quarter of the nineteenth century, were almost always the work of groups. Raffle quilts made to raise money for a church or hospital are frequently the work of members of an auxiliary or guild. Many organizations have discovered that it is necessary to have an overseer for such a group project to inspect the work and keep it uniform. Frequently there is also a designer and one theme, with the result that it becomes almost impossible to distinguish a really fine group quilt from one produced by a single skilled quilter.

The idea of group quilts has spread, and as quilt guilds expand and multiply, new formulas are developed. Each person in a guild often has a chance to collect blocks from all the other members — on her birthday, as a

Group quilt made by the Ladies Society, First Presbyterian Church, 12 West 12th Street, New York City, in 1891. It depicts the Brooklyn Bridge, flags of forty-eight states, and insignia of eighty-six D.A.R. posts. Also included are the signatures of Benjamin Harrison, members of his cabinet, and forty-three governors. It was raffled as a fund-raiser and eventually presented to Margaret Clarke Goodall Bradley, one of the dedicated workers on the project. 106 x 107". Courtesy of The Smithsonian Institution, Washington, D.C. Gift of Emily Noakes Manley

A wool quilt of suitings and other scrap fabric is sometimes called a "hap," especially in Pennsylvania and related areas. This one from the Shenandoah Valley, Virginia, was made in 1900 by Anna Jeannette Baker. Collection of Nancy Johnson

result of a drawing, or as outgoing president of the group. It is easy to invent reasons for exchanging blocks, in order that each member may have a quilt representing her friends in that group. The rules usually stipulate that the recipient can choose her own pattern or patterns, colors, or even certain fabrics, so that the finished quilt will look planned and perfect rather than haphazard. A group quilt can also be made as a surprise for a member, with the design and colors chosen by friends who are apt to know her taste in quilts.

See also: Album quilts, Baltimore album quilts, Brides' quilts, Cause quilts, Friendship quilts, Guilds, Presentation quilts

GUILDS

Originally, guilds were organizations of workers in specific fields, such as silversmiths or cobblers. The word has come to mean groups of people interested in a common purpose, not necessarily for financial gain. Quilters, especially, have used this word to describe their organizations.

Though quilting died out in the period from World War II to the Bicentennial, there are guilds that have met continuously for as long as seventy-five years. In this present quilting renaissance, new guilds have formed, many of them splitting into smaller groups when their numbers become too large. There are also very large umbrella groups, like The New England Quilters' Guild with over fifteen hundred members.

Some guilds have large enough treasuries to enable them to award scholarships, support research projects, and finance other worthwhile endeavors. Many have also produced quilts in quantity for children's hospi-

tals, nursing homes, and shelters for abused women. They also frequently produce group quilts for sale or raffle to raise funds for their charitable work.

See also: Group quilts, Friendship quilts, Fund-raiser quilts, State quilt projects

HAPS

Rough wool utility quilts, often tied rather than quilted, were known as "haps" in central Pennsylvania and some other country areas. The origin of this Middle English word is somewhat obscure but it appears to have been used in northern England to describe a utility cover of rough material.

See also: Utility quilts, Wool

HAWAIIAN QUILTS

The great allover appliqué quilts of Hawaii seem to have sprung full blown from the minds of the talented island women. Although it is true that the missionaries in the midnineteenth century brought new types of fabric and needlework with them to

the Hawaiian Islands, the quilts that they first taught the islanders to make were the same simple pieced and appliqué designs that came with them from New England.

The Hawaiians' love of nature and of flowing design blossomed into a truly new type of quilt, with one huge appliqué design spreading out to sides and corners from an elaborate center. The pattern is created with a paper-fold technique, in much the way a child's cutout string of paper dolls is made, except that a square is used and folded across in both directions and once again from the corner to form eight layers. Each woman created her own designs, usually based on fruits, flowers, and leaves, and often passed them on to her daughters. We now see the ideas and style used in wall hangings as well as in full-size bed quilts following the original designs. Not only have the designs influenced quilts beyond Hawaii, but so has the actual turning and stitching technique used for the intricate curves — it is referred to as "Hawaiian

appliqué." The background quilting follows the outline of the appliqué design and is called wave, or echo, quilting.

The other type of quilt designed and made by Hawaiian women is the patriotic flag quilt. These were first seen around the turn of the century and can now be found in many museums both in the islands and on the mainland.

See also: Appliqué, Flag quilts

HEART MOTIFS

Quilters have always found the heart an appealing design element. It is simple to draw or to cut from folded paper; it can be worked in appliqué or embroidery, or stitched like a secret message in the quilting. Pennsylvania quilters work hearts into almost any design. In recent years, the teacher and writer Karen O'Dowd has used heart motifs as her identifying mark. She

LEFT: A typical Hawaiian appliqué quilt in one color on white. The designs for these quilts were traditionally made and cut individually, using a paper-fold method, and they were rarely shared by the designer/maker. 84 x 92". Collection of Susan Parrish, Antiques

BELOW: Heart designs are used for wedding quilts, for gifts to daughters and dear friends, and probably were made as a relief from the straight lines of pieced quilt designs. This pieced and appliquéd quilt is from the late nineteenth century. 68 x 92". Collection of Thos. K. Woodard: American Antiques & Quilts. (Detail)

A detail of a large Hmong Pa nDau or flower cloth, meaning any piece of fabric decorated with any embroidery. The designs are largely traditional and are used over and over in varying combinations. The center design in the block is called a fletch or arrow feather. Around that are snail houses with small diamonds, used to create a sparkling effect. The repeating starlike lines make a spiderweb. Whole piece, 110 x 128". Collection of the author

OPPOSITE PAGE: Hosanna was designed by Joyce Schlotzhauer in 1979 to celebrate the religious significance of Christmas. It was created by a group of six women — Romayne Bonk, Nancy Drum, Betty Havlik, Cassie Heib, Maxine Lorey, and Mrs. Schlotzhauer. 62 x 62". Collection of Rev. Dr. and Mrs. James W. Muir

has created designs with them for every occasion and for every season of the year and has written a small book showing exactly how to use hearts creatively in more than a dozen quilts.

See also: Holiday themes

HEXAGONS

One of the most versatile of all geometric shapes is the hexagon. It can be cut up and fitted back together with many other 60° and 120° shapes, such as the equilateral triangle and the 60° diamond. Early tiles and mosaics from the Mediterranean area were composed of hexagons and their related shapes. The staple of English quilting from the eighteenth century until today has been the paper-pieced tiny hexagon.

Grandmother's Flower Garden is a pattern dear to the twentieth-century American quilter, who relied on the clever use of scrap fabric for design variations.

See also: English piecing, Geometry, Grandmother's Flower Garden, Mosaics

HMONG NEEDLEWORK

The Hmong (pronounced "mung") people from the mountain regions of Laos, Thailand, and Vietnam have settled in this country in large numbers in recent years, bringing with them a wealth of beautiful needlework. The technique of interest to quilters is a form of reverse appliqué in two and sometimes three colors and formal geometric design. Fine bedspreads, backed but not batted, are available at craft shows and in some museum shops. Smaller pieces and some clothing are also made for the American market. Appliqué, alone or in combination with expert cross-stitch and other

embroidery, is called *pa ndau* ("pondouw") by the Hmong people. The word means "flower cloth."

See also: Reverse appliqué

HOLIDAY THEMES

Christmas, Valentine's Day, and the Fourth of July rate high among the holidays that quilters celebrate in their designs. Some homes now have Christmas quilts for every bed in the house, used only during that short season of the year. The many red-and-green quilts from the nineteenth century were not necessarily intended for Christmas, but others can be found with designs of stars, poinsettia, and pine trees that are certainly appropriate for that occasion. More recent designs include Santa, angels, and even Rudolph the Red-Nosed Reindeer.

Valentine quilts, lavished with hearts, and Fourth of July motifs with flags are more often confined to the small wall-hanging variety. There have been several series of patterns made for such decorative quilts for each month of the year, covering holidays like Halloween and Easter.

See also: Flag quilts, Heart motifs, Tree motifs

HOMESPUN

The use of the word "homespun" is somewhat confusing, as it is often taken to mean "hand-woven" or "woven at home." Before cotton became the universal fabric of America, many people raised the sheep, grew the flax, spun the thread, and wove the fabric used by the family. Early cotton fabrics were sometimes produced entirely at home by hand.

"Homespun" actually refers to the entire

Homespun quilt, probably for a bride, made in the early nineteenth century in New England. The hearts, flowers, pomegranates, and vines are all motifs found on wedding quilts. 99 x 79". Collection of the American Museum in Britain, Claverton Manor, Bath, England. Gift of Mrs. Nancy Lancaster

production of a piece of fabric, both the spinning and the weaving. The word also was used for types of heavy cotton fabrics that only appeared to have been handwoven.

By the end of the eighteenth century, imported and locally manufactured goods were prevalent, though perhaps in wilderness areas it was a necessity to produce one's own cloth. Very little of the commercial "homespun" found its way into quilts, however. The exceptions are some backings, of linen or wool, on fine chintz or glazed wool quilts, and very occasionally an entire wool quilt, top and back. A true "homespun" quilt is, indeed, an unusual treasure.

See also: Linen, Linsey-woolsey, Wool

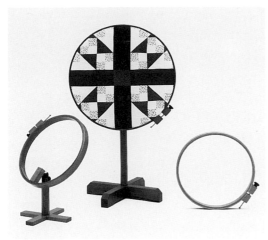

HOOPS

The alternative to quilting on a large frame is to quilt on a hand-held hoop. This is usually made of wood and is constructed exactly like a large embroidery hoop. The three layers of the quilt are first pinned or basted together and then the hoop is moved from one area to another as the quilting is finished.

See also: Frames, Quilting

I

IDENTIFICATION

All antiques and other collectibles must be identified with some certainty before a value can be set — and quilts are no different. If a quilt is signed and dated by the maker, part of the battle is won. A label with additional information, such as locale or the purpose of the quilt — a gift or raffle, for example — can solve the problem of identification very easily. Without these aids, it is necessary to know the period when the fabric was manufactured, the type of batting, and many other clues. The state quilt projects have been very helpful in identifying quilts and making their value far easier to assess.

See also: Appraisals, Fabrics, Labels, Signing, State quilt projects

INDIAN INFLUENCE (AMERICAN)

Native American design, often geometric, is so powerful, it seems perfectly suited to quilts. The blending of designs, colors, and materials of the peoples of Europe and the Americas created changes in styles and exciting effects in many crafts, but in none more than quilts. Seminole piecing is an example of Native American design worked on the sewing machine with fabrics from the new Americans.

Dr. Joyce Mori decided a few years ago to find out to what degree American Indian design had affected quilts. The earliest example that she found of such influence is in a quilt from 1889, now owned by David

LEFT: Three types of quilting hoops. From the left, a standing table hoop, a standing floor hoop, and a lap hoop

RIGHT: There are a number of clues to the identification of this quilt, starting with the Oregon Pioneer Association ribbons. It is not a state centennial commemorative quilt, as the latest dates are early 1920s. The center square has two names embroidered — the maker and the recipient. 67 x 72". Collection of the Museum of American Folk Art, New York. Gift of Margaret Cavigga

INDIAN INFLUENCE

Fran Soika is a leader in the designing of quilts from American Indian art. This wall hanging comes from a pottery design in the Albuquerque area

throughout Europe after the late seventeenth century.

See also: Chintz, Fabrics, Palampores, Tree of Life

Schorsch. She documented over four hundred other quilted articles that employed Indian designs or themes. She also discovered that there are 130 traditional quilt patterns with Indian-related names, such as Indian Hatchet, Cherokee, and Crossed Canoes.

There are several quilters currently working with Indian design themes, among them Fran Soika, Erma Martin Yost, Win Burry, and Gail Garber. Fran Soika has incorporated pottery designs into her quilts and has developed a close relationship with Native American artists in the Albuquerque area.

See also: Seminole strip piecing

INDIAN INFLUENCE (EASTERN)

The first decorated quilts were made with the beautifully printed and painted fabrics that were brought to Europe from India in the seventeenth and eighteenth centuries. The palampores with the great Tree of Life designs were used, along with other chintz designs, in the finely crafted appliqué quilts of England and America. The very importation of cotton itself — largely from India — changed the nature of clothing and bedding

INVITATIONAL SHOWS

An invitational show of quilts allows a limit to be set on size and content and assures a high quality that is not possible in a more open format. Only the juried show is comparable. An invitational show may be organized around the work of one or more quilt artists, an especially fine private collection, or a group of quilts on one theme or of one type — for example, floral designs or geometric pieced designs.

Almost all museum shows are, in one way or another, invitational. Many large shows and festivals include one judged show and several smaller invitational shows, allowing a variety to please a wider range of people.

As the popularity of quilts as a visual-art medium becomes increasingly evident, more institutions, such as schools, libraries, and commercial malls, see them as a way to attract attention and sometimes to make money. The availability of fine quilts and the familiarity of the medium to a larger public make the invitational quilt show a greater crowd pleaser than almost any other type of local art exhibit.

See also: Shows

IRISH CHAIN

There is no evidence that this crisp geometric design, either in its simplest or most complex form, ever came from Ireland. The simple Single Irish Chain is nothing more than nine-patch blocks alternated with plain blocks, creating a diagonal chain effect

across the entire surface of the quilt. Double Irish Chains are probably the most common. One of the oldest is of navy and red linsey-woolsey, in the collection of Gunston Hall in Virginia; it is said to date from before the American Revolution. A *Godey's Lady's Book* from 1849 mentions the Irish Chain pattern as something from the past. The popularity of this pattern has never faded, and it can be found in wool, silk, cotton scrap, or enhanced with fine appliqué and quilting in the open spaces.

See also: Depression quilts, Godey's Lady's Book, Linsey-woolsey, Nine-patch designs

IRISH QUILTS

Ireland did not share with England and Wales in the nineteenth-century craze for patchwork or medallion quilts. True Irish antique quilts, as seen in museums in that country, are usually all wool, similar to the whole-cloth Early American quilts. The quilting designs are generally of Celtic origin.

There is now a revival of quilting in Ireland, and fine quilts in many of today's styles are being made. There is an Irish Patchwork Society, and interest is spreading as it is in other Western countries.

See also: English quilts, Welsh quilts

J JAPANESE INFLUENCE

It could be said that the Japanese influenced quilting in the nineteenth century, when silk became a fabric of choice. Other Oriental textiles and motifs have influenced design in England and America, but in recent years there has been a marked exchange between American and Japanese quilters. In the 1970s, when Japanese women first became interested in American quilting, they often worked traditional American designs in Japanese

LEFT: Single Irish Chain with *broderie perse* centers, signed and dated, "Mar. 8, 1838. Happy Natal Day, Sophia Caroline Davenport." Shown in the Josiah Bell House. Collection of Beaufort Historical Association's Old Town Restoration, Beaufort, North Carolina

BELOW, LEFT: Japanese under-kimono with pieced Hexagon Star design and stenciled sleeve borders. This delicate wool piece from the Meiji period (nineteenth century) reflects the same geometric design ideas that Americans were increasingly incorporating into their quilts in the nineteenth and twentieth centuries. Collection of Fifi White

BELOW, RIGHT: Japanese fireman's coat with a standard design and layered cotton with *sashiko* quilting, from the late Edo period (nineteenth century). The Oriental countries were known for their textile skills, and were printing and decorating cloth long before the European countries. By the nineteenth century, pieces as elaborately worked as this utilitarian coat were commonplace. Collection of Fifi White

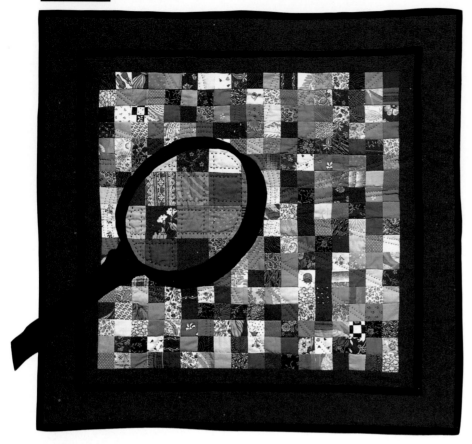

A close look at judging as seen by Betsy Freeman of North Carolina, herself a frequent judge. The amusing scrap wall quilt is correct in each detail, including the magnified black thread. 25 x 25"

OPPOSITE PAGE: The second Great American Quilt Contest, sponsored by the Museum of American Folk Art in 1989, was called Childhood Memories. The quilts from each state were first juried from slides. Two from each state were then judged for the final winners. Childhood Memory #44: The Cellar by Elaine Spencer of Colorado won first place. 45 x 54". Courtesy of the Museum of American Folk Art, New York

fabrics, achieving a very fresh look. Americans sought out Japanese fabrics and used them to advantage in original designs. In the last decade, there have been many shows that traveled between the two countries, resulting in an increased interchange of ideas.
See also: Sashiko, Tie-dyeing

JARGON

Any art, craft, or profession spawns a number of words and phrases that are at first slang, or an "in" language, but that eventually pass into legitimate usage or else disappear. In the late nineteenth century, the phrase "charm quilt" meant a quilt in which no two pieces of fabric were alike. This usage has become standard and is understood by all quilters.

In the current revival of quilting, dark quilts are often spoken of as being subject to "bearding." This means that the fibers of the white batting come out through the dark fabric, creating an unattractive fuzz on the surface. Either the problem will be solved by manufacturers, or the word will come into permanent usage.

Very old quilts that are worn beyond hope of repair or use are called "cutters." Their only future is to be cut up and some parts salvaged for vests, pillows, and stuffed toys.

"Poverty piecing" is most obvious in country quilts and especially those made in times of war and depression. Even the smallest pieces of the design are often seamed together out of miniscule bits of fabric — frequently with no attention paid to fabric direction or grain line.

An amusing phrase that may have come from country women of long ago but could only be understood by a dedicated quilter is "toenail-catcher." This refers to a badly made quilt in which the quilting stitches are so long that the users of the quilt are in danger of catching their toenails in them.
See also: Charm quilts

JUDGED SHOWS

Judged quilt shows have been an exciting part of American quilting for more than a hundred years. As the country moved westward, state-fair quilt competitions were established across the continent, and quilts and other handwork were an important division for women, along with baked goods and canning.

Quilt shows in the late twentieth century have grown in size and scope, and the judged portions have grown in importance, as the prize money often has. A panel of

Kits for juvenile quilts were popular in the 1930-40 period. This one with its European postcard designs was considered suitable for girls or boys. 62 x 41". Collection of Thos. K. Woodard: American Antiques & Quilts

judges usually works for several days ahead of the show's opening, looking at each quilt and evaluating it carefully. Judges are chosen from among a pool of knowledgeable people, with the panel including prizewinners from other years and other contests, quilting teachers, quilt magazine editors, artists, museum curators of textiles, or collectors. There are usually three people on a panel but this is not a hard and fast rule.

Some shows award very nice money prizes, others give gift certificates — usually to the local quilt shop — and others give only a ribbon, pleasing publicity, and the satisfaction of recognition by experts.
See also: Contests, Juried shows, Prizewinning quilts, Shows, State fairs

JURIED SHOWS

Judged quilt shows have been around for a long time, but juried shows have only recently become more important. Jurying, like judging, is usually done by a select panel of experts and generally precedes the in-hand judging by several weeks. It is difficult to ship so many quilts and expensive to return them, so the jurying is usually done from 35-mm slides. Along with the entry form, the entrant receives instructions about photographing and the number of slides necessary — details as well as an overall picture of the quilt are often requested.

A number of quilts are then selected for the show and the slides returned to the quilters. The selected quilts are sent in for final judging a few days ahead of the actual show. Large shows that will have printed catalogues require the quilts to be in the hands of the judges even earlier, to allow time for them to be properly photographed

and the catalogue printed. At the time of the show, the winners of the jurying will be hung, and the ribbons pinned on the few final winners chosen by the judges.
See also: Contests, Judged shows, Prizewinning quilts, Shows

JUVENILE QUILTS

Patterns and kits for children's quilts are ever-popular. They are usually labeled "Juvenile," perhaps to span the ages better than "Baby" or "Children." The themes are nursery tales, animals, and circuses, as well as the popular Sunbonnet Sue and Overall Sam designs so familiar to quilters.
See also: Children's quilts, Overall Boy, Sunbonnet Sue

KIT QUILTS

As America moved into the twentieth century, quilting became a business rather than an individual enterprise. Pattern companies competed for space in newspapers and on store shelves. Kits, completely planned and stamped, became very popular, setting styles and trends still recognizable today. Not only the cross-stitch and embroidered quilt tops, but graceful floral appliqués, tempted every needleworker to become a quilter. The best-known company in this field was Paragon, no longer in business. The only kits now are sold by large general-needlework catalogue houses like Herrschner's.

The style most characteristic of the twenties through the prewar period is the floral appliqué with a center motif and carefully planned border, often finished with a scalloped edge. All-white quilts were also popular kit items. Both of these styles are now being designed again and produced as full-size patterns.

See also: All-white quilts, Appliqué, Cross-stitching, Embroidery

LABELS

Signing or labeling any piece of embroidery or handwork enhances its interest to future generations and adds to its value when it becomes an antique. It is very easy to mark a quilt with a separate embroidered or stamped label applied to the back corner. Cross-stitching on hardanger or other even-weave fabrics makes a pretty label showing that the maker cared enough for posterity to do that extra bit of work.

ABOVE: Kit quilts were popular in the Depression; many, like this one, produced by Paragon. This is kit #7168, dated 1934. It was purchased in 1979 by Judy Linsay, appliquéd in 1981 by Cuba Tracewell, and finally quilted by Erma Kirkpatrick and a group in 1981. 91 x 71". Private collection

LEFT: A properly embroidered identification label may be put on the top of a quilt, as Bernice Enyeart has done on her Baltimore album quilt, or it may be sewed onto a corner of the quilt back. The name, date, and place are important to future generations

Heavy cotton lace was a popular edging for Victorian crazy quilts. This one has the initials A.L.C. in the border (seen here), and in another place A.L.H. There are several hearts throughout the design and the name Willet Hall, leading to the conjecture that it might be a wedding quilt. Collection of the author. (Detail)

Designs and alphabets for such labels can be found in a number of books.

See also: Identification, Signature quilts, Signing

LACE

The quilts of the late Victorian period were often made of extravagant fabrics and trimmed in like manner. An edging of heavy cream-colored lace was not unusual on silk and velvet quilts.

See also: Edging, Victorian crazy quilts

LAP QUILTING

Television has brought quilting classes into the homes of millions of Americans. One of the best-known teachers is Georgia Bonesteel, recognized for her easy lap-quilting technique. The method has been around for years and has been called variously quilt-as-you-go and block-by-block quilting. Each block is completed, including backing, batting, and quilting, and then joined to the other finished blocks in such a way that the end product looks exactly like any quilt made by conventional methods. Lap quilting is especially well suited to any block designs, pieced or appliqué, or to any quilt top that can be broken into smaller units.

See also: Block-by-block, Quilt-as-you-go

LINEN

Before cotton became common in Europe in the late seventeenth century, linen was the summer alternative to wool. The long and demanding process of removing the fiber from the stalks of flax was known in Mediterranean countries several thousand years ago.

Though early bed coverings were made of linen, it is not found in many quilts of the nineteenth or even the late eighteenth century. A few printed linens, including commemorative handkerchiefs, appear in medallion quilts, and quilt backings were sometimes of coarse linen.

See also: Backings, Fabrics

LININGS

In general, the fabric on the reverse side of a quilt is referred to as "backing." Very heavy and highly decorative pieces such as Victorian crazy quilts are finished with a lining of

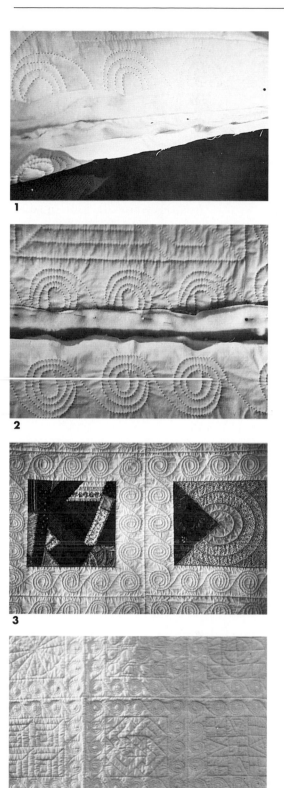

1

2

3

4

satin or sateen, which is then tacked through to the top to hold it in place.
See also: Backings, Victorian crazy quilts

LINSEY-WOOLSEY

The word "linsey-woolsey" may at one time have meant a specific type of wool fabric, defined by weave or fiber content. Since the seventeenth century, when many wool quilts were made; the exact meaning of the word has become blurred. It could have had one of two origins — the most likely being the fact of its having been manufactured first in the town of Linsey, England. It also seems frequently to have had a linen warp thread, later cotton, for added strength. Almost any rough woolen fabric used in quilts is now referred to as "linsey-woolsey."
See also: Glazed fabrics, Linen, Wool

LITERARY MOTIFS

Not only individual quilters, but large pattern companies in their search for pictorial inspiration, have borrowed from literature. Especially in the area of children's quilts and crib quilts there are familiar figures like Humpty-Dumpty and Jack and Jill. Even Walt Disney figures have been used, but they cannot, of course, be used for the commercial market without proper licensing. Ancient myths, fairy tales, and medieval books are in the public domain and therefore their characters are available.
See also: Design sources

LOG CABIN

A favorite quilt pattern is the strip-pieced Log Cabin. The origin of this simple yet versatile arrangement may have some connection with the presidency of Abraham

Series showing lap quilting or block-by-block quilting. **1.** Edge of a quilted block with the backing turned away from the seam that is pinned through the other two layers. **2.** The back of two blocks with seam pinned and trimmed. **3.** Front of quilt, showing seams between blocks. **4.** Detail of back of quilt with seams smoothly hand-finished. Courtesy of Georgia Bonesteel

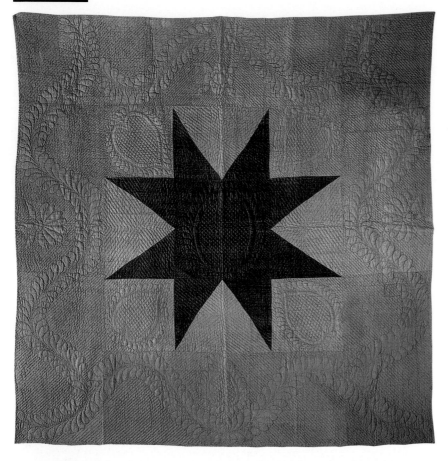

Lincoln, as the earliest known examples were made in the 1860s.

In the latter part of the nineteenth century, many Log Cabin quilts were made by the foundation method, with a muslin base the size of each block. Many of these were of silk, wool, or a combination of the two. In some Log Cabins of this period the strips were folded and then laid down, creating a three-dimensional effect. It also created more thickness than the muslin base alone. For this reason, many late-nineteenth-century Log Cabins are not batted but are backed and tied in the manner of Victorian crazy quilts.

As Victorian quilts of wool and silk fell slowly out of favor in the twentieth century, Log Cabins were more often made of cotton prints and pieced with a running-stitch seam, either by hand or machine. They are now favored for scrap piecing and for quick cutting in layers, as all of the pieces are the same width and can be cut into any length and then cut off into the specific length required by the design.

There are several variations of the basic Log Cabin. The White House Steps and Court House Steps are the simplest, the eight-sided Pineapple is the most complex. *See also: Foundation piecing, Pineapples, Strip piecing, Victorian crazy quilts*

MARKING

The problems of marking a quilting design on a white surface so that it can be seen by the quilter but will not remain permanently on the quilt are discussed whenever quilters get together. A hard lead pencil has been the choice of most quilters through

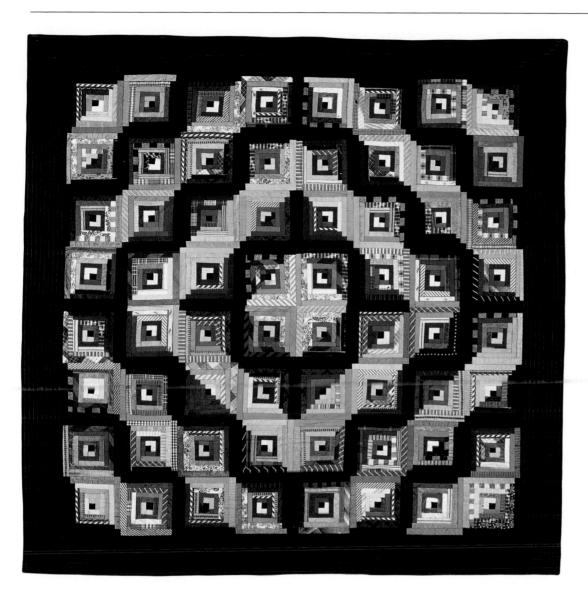

OPPOSITE PAGE, TOP: Linsey-woolsey from New England, 1815-25. The large pieced star is fairly unusual in a quilt of this type, typically of whole cloth. The wool is slightly glazed. 100 x 99". Collection of the Museum of American Folk Art, New York. Gift of Cyril Nelson

OPPOSITE PAGE, BOTTOM: Log Cabin in one of many Sunshine and Shadows variations. This is a typical midwest Amish wool and cotton quilt of the early twentieth century. 71 x 62". Collection of the Museum of American Folk Art, New York. Gift of David Pottinger

LEFT: Log Cabin in the most familiar Barn Raising arrangement, made by Sarah Olmstead King of Connecticut in the nineteenth century. The interesting selection of silks, velvets, and ribbons was typical of the Victorian period. 66 x 66". Collection of the Museum of American Folk Art, New York. Gift of Mrs. E. Regan Kerney

the years, as it remains visible for as long as it takes to quilt the entire piece yet is not noticeable afterward. Some pencil marking can be removed with an art gum eraser and some will wash out.

In recent years several new marking pens have come on the market. Each one seems to have advantages and drawbacks, so trial, error, and discussion among quilters has been beneficial both to quilters and manufacturers. Narrow masking tape is an effective guide for straight-line quilting.

For many years there were women and men who only marked quilt tops for other people to quilt. So many quilters now consider the quilting an integral part of the design that they prefer to mark it themselves, even when they hire someone to do the quilting.

An entire business has grown up around patterns for quilting designs. There are stencils and templates that can be placed on the surface and drawn around. There are also large designs printed boldly on white paper; these are laid under the quilt top, often over a light box, and traced.

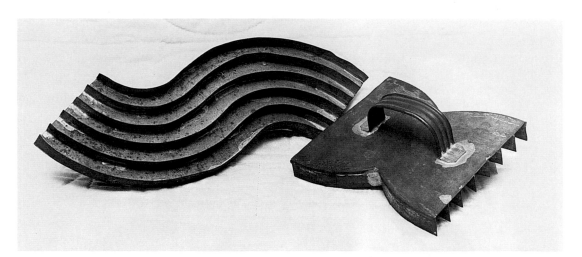

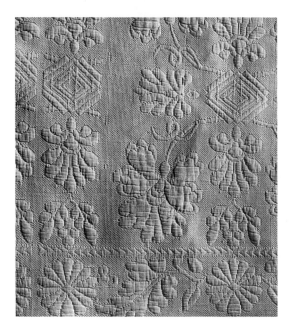

Kits and preprinted whole-cloth quilt tops presented one major and seemingly insurmountable problem. The quilting was marked with blue dots that did not rub off in handling or during quilting — unfortunately they did not wash out after quilting, either. A new printing process now allows for very fine preprinted whole-cloth tops called Doublestencil™ Kits & Fabrics; the marking is guaranteed to wash out.
See also: Quilting, Whole-cloth quilts

MARRIAGE QUILTS

A marriage or wedding quilt is usually made for a bride or a couple as a wedding present. It may be made by a group or by the bride's or groom's mother or sister, and usually displays traditional symbols or designs, such as Bridal Bouquet.
See also: Brides' quilts, Wedding Ring

MARSEILLES SPREADS

The true Marseilles counterpane, or spread, is not a quilt at all, but a machine-made, all-white fabric with a raised design that looks a little like trapunto. These were first made in the last quarter of the eighteenth century on a jacquard-type loom. Up until that time,

what is sometimes called Marseilles quilting — whole-cloth or all-white — had been produced by hand, so that an entire small industry was threatened by the mechanization. Probably because white is an attractive choice for almost any bedroom, both the Marseilles spreads and the elegant all-white quilts handmade in the North of England were popular through the nineteenth century. In America in Victorian times the Marseilles spread was an essential of any well-furnished house.
See also: All-white quilts, Trapunto

MEDALLION QUILTS

The carefully planned quilts with center panels and surrounding borders are called medallion quilts. Many of the finest eighteenth- and nineteenth-century English quilts were made in this style — an excellent collection of them can be seen in the Victoria and Albert Museum in London.

Americans used the same chintzes and other fine cottons that the English did dur-

ing the late eighteenth and early nineteenth centuries. They also copied the styles of the English quilts, so many Early American quilts are also in the medallion design. The historical handkerchief prints that commemorated great personages and great events were often used for the center panels. For this reason medallion quilts again became popular at the time of the Centennial, when there were many such handkerchiefs printed.

Nearly a hundred years later, Jinny Beyer, a well-known designer and quiltmaker, popularized the medallion quilt once more. Her use of dark fabrics and star patterns gave her medallions a sophisticated decorator appearance. She wrote a book called *Medallion Quilts*, which, with the classes she teaches, has helped other quilters to work out and use medallion designs.
See also: English quilts

MEMORY QUILTS

Women seem always to have enjoyed recording events, as in the little memory books dear to high school girls of another era. Memory quilts celebrate times, places, occasions, or groups of people that a woman wishes to keep close. She may make the entire quilt from her own design — for example, a picture of a place connected with some event in her life. She may make a sort of sampler, using blocks with names related to her experiences, such as Pine Tree and Moon Over the Mountain for an especially beloved vacation spot. Sometimes writing is included in the quilt, poems or identifications of some sort. Memory quilts are also made by groups as a gift to a member.
See also: Album quilts, Friendship quilts

OPPOSITE PAGE, TOP: A simple medallion quilt with a basket center and delicate appliqué leaf-and-flower borders with tiny inset bands of sawtooth piecing. It was made in the midnineteenth century and belonged to George Slothower of Baltimore, Maryland. 92 x 93″. Courtesy of The Smithsonian Institution, Washington, D.C. Gift of Miss Doris E. Slothower

OPPOSITE PAGE, BOTTOM: Welsh medallion quilt, early twentieth century. The simplicity of the medallion makes an excellent background for the beautiful Welsh quilting designs. Collection of Peggy Wanamaker

LEFT: Valerie Fons and her husband-to-be, Verlen Kruger, set a world's record for canoeing the 2,348-mile length of the Mississippi. Valerie and her sister-in-law, Marienne Fons, made this quilt to commemorate the accomplishment. The names of the blocks all have to do with stages and memories of the trip: Crossed Canoes, Wild Waves, Swamp Patch, and the Fish Block, to name a few. 86 x 110″

MEN AS QUILTERS

Men have always been interested in quilting, though it has been predominantly a woman's occupation. In seventeenth-century England, quiltmakers were members of the textile trade, and the work was done by both women and men. There is an English song from the early nineteenth century, "Old Joe the Quilter," about an actual, documented man who made his living at quilting.

There are many family stories about men who designed or cut the pieces for the quilts

their wives made. Some men, especially farmers who found themselves housebound for long hours in the winter, gradually took up quilting — possibly because it looked as though their wives were having more fun than they were. One astonishingly prolific farmer-quilter in the twentieth century was Ernie Haight of Nebraska, known as "the father of machine quilting."

In the current revival of quilting, some of the best-known designers and innovators are men, among them Michael James and Jeffrey Gutcheon. The team of Joe Cunningham and Gwen Marston is famous for teaching, writing, and setting trends in a rather traditional form of quilting. Hollis Turnbow has renown as a quilter, but especially as a producer of quilting designs.

MENNONITE QUILTS

It is easy for most "English" (as the Mennonites call them), or non-German-speaking, Americans to confuse the Amish and the Mennonites. Indeed their lifestyles are similar but, in general, the Mennonites live in a more modern fashion. Their turn-of-the-century quilts are very much like those of the Amish of the same period, however, using plain, dark colors and simple designs.

As time went on, the Mennonites copied more from their "English" neighbors and added brighter colors and more prints. Unless the history of a specific quilt is known, it is much harder to identify a quilt as Mennonite than as Amish.

The main thrust of Mennonite quilting today is the production of quilts for the large auctions held in Pennsylvania, the Midwest, and the Shenandoah Valley of Virginia. Almost all the proceeds of these sales

go to the Mennonite Central Committee for their world relief program. There are other, individual Mennonite quilt sales and auctions, such as the one for the Sunshine Home for children in Ohio. The Amish and Mennonite women work together as well as separately all winter to make quilts for these numerous causes. Some patterns, such as the Giant Dahlia and the Country Bride, are ever-popular staples and have come to be thought of as Mennonite quilts.

See also: Amish quilts

MINIATURE QUILTS

As wall quilts become more and more popular, quilters looking for new challenges have made miniature quilts for decorative purposes. A miniature is not a doll quilt but a

OPPOSITE PAGE: James Williams, a tailor of Wrexham, Denbighshire, Wales, completed this magnificent work of art in 1852. At the top are the symbols of four British countries and a crown. The center designs are mostly Biblical, combined with contemporary engineering wonders like the Cefn Viaduct, completed in 1848. Though the maker was a fine tailor and craftsman, he was an untutored artist — it took ten years to complete this work. 82 x 90″. Collection of the Welsh Folk Museum, St. Fagans, Wales

ABOVE: Pennsylvania Mennonite Feathered Star quilt, ca. 1890. Until recent years the Mennonites made dark quilts in traditional patterns similar to many of the better-known Amish quilts. Collection of America Hurrah, New York City

perfectly scaled replica of a large quilt. When photographed, it must be shown with familiar objects for scale or it can be mistaken for a full-size quilt.
See also: Doll quilts, Wall quilts

MOLAS

The women of the Cuna-Cuna or San Blas Indian tribe of the north coast of Panama make and wear colorful blouses with back and front appliqué panels called *molas*. The color, technique, and style of these striking pieces of needlework have made them popular with collectors in recent years. The appliqué is a reverse process through layers of different colors, each color being revealed as a single bright outline when the layer above is cut away. Many of the designs are similar to Pop Art, depicting the emblems from cigarette packs, myths, and news of the day. No theme is too grand or too trivial to be worked into the small area of a mola.
See also: Appliqué, Hmong needlework, Reverse appliqué

MOSAICS

Continuous hexagon designs are sometimes called mosaics. This most versatile shape can be used to create floral designs, baskets, and intricate abstract arrangements, just as the ancient Mediterranean tiles or mosaics were. The most common arrangement is Grandmother's Flower Garden.
See also: Geometry, Grandmother's Flower Garden, Hexagons

MOURNING QUILTS

In today's world the idea of a mourning quilt seems odd to most people, but in the nineteenth century death and mourning were an accepted part of everyday life. Families were large, and people died young of diseases that have all but disappeared. Women frequently had mourning wardrobes ready for the next sad occasion. The dresses were often elegant, and the accessories — parasols, handbags, and jewelry — were black as well.

Well-to-do needleworkers created

exquisite silk mourning pictures during the mourning period, when they often did not venture out socially. A woman who made quilts for her family would naturally mark the death of a member with a piece of her handwork. These quilts are often rewarding for researchers, because they have birth and death dates and other interesting and pertinent family information.

See also: Identification, Researchers and historians

Mourning quilt made by Nancy Ward Butler of Jamestown, New York, to mark the death of her grandchild, Nancy A. Butler, in 1842. The letters and numbers are appliqué, the borders are pieced. 79 x 80". Courtesy of The Smithsonian Institution, Washington, D.C. Gift of Nancy A. Butler Werdell

MUSEUMS

Very few museums started out with the avowed purpose of collecting quilts. They have either focused on folk art or textiles — and quilts are an obvious part of those fields — or the museums have started a quilt collection quite unintentionally with the donation of a private or family bequest. As the artistic and monetary value of quilts becomes more recognized, museums now actively seek quilts as an important part of their collections.

The Smithsonian Institution has one of the finest collections of American quilts in the country, and its origins are fairly representative. Just before 1900, a group of textiles from the Copp family of Stonington, Connecticut, was given to the museum by John Brenton Copp III. Among the pieces were the first three quilts to be housed in the museum. This was not, in today's sense, a collection, but actual family pieces used between 1750 and 1850. They were typical of the household goods and clothing of a prosperous but not wealthy family from New England.

The Museum of American Folk Art has a fine quilt collection, many of whose pieces are pictured in this volume. The D.A.R. Museum in Washington, D.C., is also proud of a collection of mostly Early American quilts. The Valentine Museum in Richmond, Virginia, has an extensive textile collection, including many quilts.

Museums that offer a total immersion in Americana certainly must include quilts. Three of the best-known of these are the Shelburne in Vermont, Living History Farms in Iowa, and the Henry Ford Museum and Greenfield Village, outside Detroit.

State museums often have fine quilt collections. The Indiana State Museum and the Minnesota Historical Society have well-documented collections showing the quilts of their respective areas. The trend for the future in state and local museums is to concentrate on those quilts made by or connected with local families.

There are several museums in England that house major quilt collections. Interestingly, one of these is composed entirely of American quilts — the American Museum in Bath. The Victoria and Albert Museum has the finest collection of English quilts and other textiles, not to be missed by anyone interested in any form of textile art.

Several art museums have quilt collections. Three that are justly proud of theirs and often have them on display are the Denver Art Museum, the Museum of Fine Arts, Boston, and the Baltimore Museum of Art. Some art museums starting collections are searching for examples of specific quilts.

In recent years, three museums devoted entirely to quilts and quilters have been founded, one in the East and two in the West. The newest is the American Quilt Research Center, a division of the Los Angeles County Museum of Art. Also in California is the American Museum of Quilts and Textiles in San José — some part of the collection is always on display, and the museum also houses traveling collections. The New England Quilt Museum in Lowell, Massachusetts, is new and depends largely on touring shows or loans, though they have a small but growing permanent collection and a good collection of books and research material.

It is impossible to give an idea of the range of quilts in museums in America, but it is safe to say that many very small historical societies and houses from coast to coast have excellent, if sometimes poorly documented, quilt collections. For the researcher who wants to be in touch with the best of these and all the larger museums, there is a book by Lisa Turner Oshins of the American Folklife Center of the Library of Congress, published in 1987 by Acropolis Books, Inc., called *Quilt Collections: A Directory for the United States and Canada*.
See also: American quilts, Collectors, English quilts, Folk-art quilts

MUSLIN

Many basic, plain-weave cotton fabrics have been called "muslin" over the years. There are printed muslins and plain, but among today's quilters, white and unbleached muslins are the most familiar. All-cotton is preferred, and is used mainly as background fabric for appliqué, for the white areas in piecing, and for quilt backing. The unbleached is a gentle cream white, blending well with a large range of colors and prints.

Originally, muslin came to Europe from India. The name was used for many different cotton fabrics of many different weights. The French word is *mousseline*, and there were fabrics called *mousseline de laine* (a thin, soft wool) and *mousseline de soie* (a thin, smooth silk). Most dictionaries and books on textiles say that the word came from the name of the town of Mosul in what is now Iraq.

Nineteenth-century books refer sometimes to "sprigged muslin" as a fabric used in ladies' summer dresses. Decorated with small, fairly random floral prints, it was a fabric much used in quilts of the late nineteenth and early twentieth centuries.
See also: Cotton

NEEDLES

From the earliest bone needles used by primitive people the world over to today's sharp and inexpensive steel needles, the shape and principle of the fundamental

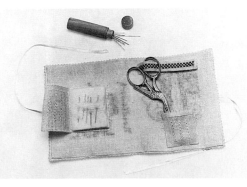

Quilters usually prefer the small, short needles called "betweens". These should be stored carefully in wooden needle tubes, needle books, or cases with wool pages that prevent rust

sewing implement has changed very little. Before there was steel, bronze and other metals were used, and as fabrics were made finer, the needles with which they were sewn had to be more versatile. Steel needles seem to have traveled from Damascus to Spain and from there, with Catherine of Aragon, to England. The best needles available still come from England.

Today, needles are usually sold in packets identified by their style and purpose — Embroidery, Crewel, or Upholstery, for example. Quilters use small needles called "betweens" in a very fine size. The size is designated by number — the larger the number, the finer the needle. A size 8 is acceptable for quilting, but many quilters use needles as fine as a size 12.

See also: Quilting, Thread

NEWSPAPER PATTERNS

Pattern companies flourished in the first half of the twentieth century, producing a wide variety of needlework and quilt designs at very reasonable prices. Newspapers and weeklies joined the parade and ran patterns, or pictures from which patterns could be ordered. The names of *Capper's Weekly, Grit,* and most of all the *Kansas City Star,* appear as sources of many patterns, not all of which were original with the publication that printed them. As a matter of fact, thorough studies of the origins of patterns have revealed that frequently the same pattern appeared with different names in at least two publications between 1925 and 1960.

See also: Patterns, Pattern companies

A Kitten pattern from Laura Wheeler, a New York syndicate name for patterns that were available throughout the country in local newspapers. The fabrics and colors are typical of the 1930-40 period, as is the use of black thread for a very showy appliqué stitch. 82 x 68". Collection of the Museum of American Folk Art, New York

NINE-PATCH DESIGNS

The nine-patch patterns are so numerous that it would be nearly impossible to list them all. The division of a block into nine squares, three in each direction, can be used to form different effects simply by the way the dark and light colors are used. The squares can also be cut across into two rectangles or from corner to corner to form triangles, permitting the design possibilities to multiply endlessly. One of the simplest yet most delightful patterns is the Single Irish Chain, formed by five dark squares and four light ones in the nine-patch blocks, which are then set alternately with all light blocks with a dark square in each corner.

See also: Four-patch designs, Irish Chain, Patterns

O CTAGONS

Several well-known quilt patterns are based on eight-sided blocks, the most popular being the Eight-Point Star. Octagons are not as easy to fit together with other shapes as are hexagons, but they can be alternated with squares, right-angle triangles, and some rectangles.
See also: Geometry, Triangles

ONE-PATCH DESIGNS

The most basic quilts are made up of same-size squares of fabric set together in rows. By careful arrangement of color and shading, interesting designs such as Sun and Shadow can be made with this one-patch system. Other one-patch designs are made up of triangles (Path Through the Woods), 60° diamonds (Tumbling Blocks), and hexagons (Grandmother's Flower Garden).
See also: Four-patch designs, Hexagons, Nine-patch designs, Triangles

ORGANIZATIONS

As quilting has become important to more people in the last quarter of the twentieth century, larger and larger organizations devoted to the craft have developed. The oldest is The National Quilting Association, incorporated in 1970. The membership in all fifty states has reached nine thousand, divided into chapters; there are also some international members. N.Q.A. publishes a national newspaper, *The Patchwork Patter,* and has certification programs for teachers and judges. The annual N.Q.A. show is held in a different city each year.

Smaller but growing organizations include the American International Quilt Association with headquarters in Houston, Texas. The membership stretches from England, Ireland, and the European continent to New Zealand, Australia, and Japan. Another growing organization with nationwide membership is the American Quilt Study Group. Their special focus is on research and history. Each year they publish a sizeable volume of research papers under the title "Uncoverings."

There are several regional umbrella guilds, probably the largest of them being The New England Quilt Guild. Its nearly two thousand members are divided into seventy local chapters.
See also: Guilds

OVERALL BOY

The original primers illustrated with Sunbonnet Babies and Children depicted exclusively girls — the enduring Sunbonnet Sue, chief among them. Quilt patterns in the early twentieth century also focused on little-girl quilts. In an effort to attract a wider audience and to vary the style and activities of the children, patternmakers invented an Overall Boy sometime in the 1920s. He

LEFT: A one-patch is the simplest of all quilt plans — random same-size squares of fabric sewn together in any pleasing and colorful arrangement. This midwestern Amish one, from about 1920-40, is quilted with a charming eight-point star design in each block. 76 x 66″. Collection of the Museum of American Folk Art, New York. Gift of David Pottinger

BELOW: Overall Boy crib quilt, designed and made by Patricia Cox for her One-of-a Kind Pattern Co. 45 x 60″

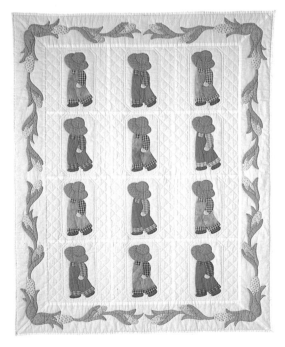

goes by various names: Overall Sam, Overall Bill, and in Jean Ray Laury's books about Sunbonnet Sue, he is Overall Andy.

Betty Hagerman of Kansas, a devotee of Sunbonnet Children, collected information and patterns. In 1978 she made a quilt called A Meeting of Sunbonnet Children. She also wrote a small book of the same name, now out of print. A fine collection of patterns for both Sunbonnet Sue and Overall Bill is published by Patricia Cox's One-of-a-Kind Designs.

See also: Appliqué, Children's quilts, Juvenile quilts, Sunbonnet Sue

PAISLEY

One of the most enduring print motifs for fabric is the intricate paisley, based on traditional Indian textile designs but taking its name from Paisley, Scotland. The textile trade with India brought to England elaborately patterned and very costly cashmere shawls that set a style. The Indian motifs, stemming from the pine cone, have enjoyed a long popularity in a wide range of fabrics all over the world. In 1808 the manufacture of large shawls started in Paisley, and the fashion continued into the late nineteenth century. A standard design printed on wool, silk, cotton, or blends came to be known as a "paisley" print. It appears in quilts from the early nineteenth century until today, and is still especially popular for men's ties.
See also: Fabrics

PALAMPORES

Palampores were painted and printed bedcovers imported into England probably from Palampur, India, in the seventeenth century. The design was Eastern, coming originally from Persia, but after palampores became popular in England, the prints were influenced by Western taste (as were export china and various trade items from the East).

Other cotton fabrics from India were called "calico" (after the Indian port of Calicut) and "chints" (now chintz), but are not identical to the fabrics bearing similar names today. The colorful designs, described as "painted" and "printed," were far more elaborate than anything created in western Europe at that time.

The first palampores were certainly too rare and expensive for the average English household, and it is thought that even in wealthier homes they were used until the background fabric began to wear out. At that time the best parts of the printed tree were cut out and applied to new fabric. Some were then backed and quilted, and some were finished as summer coverlets.
See also: Summer coverlets, Tree of Life

PAPER PIECING

Paper piecing or string piecing is sometimes confused with English piecing. Though both use a paper template, they are quite different, and the paper serves a different purpose. In string or paper piecing, the pattern shape, with seam allowance, is cut from newspaper or old letters, whichever is at hand. The first strip of fabric is laid wrong side down on the end of the pattern piece. The next piece of fabric is laid right side

The appliqué pieces on this eighteenth-century Tree of Life bedspread are typical of those cut from worn palampores and other costly India print fabrics too good to discard. The background fabric is handwoven linen. Courtesy of the Shelburne Museum, Shelburne, Vermont

down over the first piece and stitched, forming a seam through the paper. That piece of fabric is then turned over so it is wrong side down on the paper and the process is repeated. The strips — or "strings" — are usually of uneven width.

By continuing to lay strips down and seam them in place, the entire paper pattern is covered. The fabric is then trimmed around the edges to the exact shape of the pattern. When the paper is torn away the piece, made up of random strips of fabric

stitched together, can be handled as any solid fabric piece would be. Quilts made in this way are called string quilts or strip-pieced quilts.

See also: English piecing, String piecing, Strip piecing

PATCHWORK

In an art or craft such as quilting, terms change, and meanings get blurred with time and use. "Patchwork" was used in the late eighteenth and early nineteenth centuries to

A Victorian crazy quilt with the map of the United States worked in silk and velvet must have been a show of patriotism. Some of the states were still only territories when this quilt was made in 1886, in the Maryland-Virginia area. 82 x 78". Collection of the Museum of American Folk Art, New York. Gift of Dr. and Mrs. David McLaughlin

mean decorative work made up of small pieces or patches of fabric. The phrase "patchwork appliqué" is occasionally found in writings of that period. Certainly appliqué is often done with small leftover scraps and even used to cover up or patch a worn place in a garment or table linen. In America patchwork is now understood to mean pieced items.

See also: Appliqué, Pieced quilts

PATRIOTIC QUILTS

Women have used their needlework skills in the same way other artists have used their mediums — to express patriotic fervor and

to back their candidates. The large format of a quilt and the flexibility of appliqué have allowed a wide range of sentiments to be brought to life.

The major museum collections all have early quilts depicting eagles and flags. There are a number of quilts with portraits of favorite political candidates and campaign slogans. Wars and the suffrage and temperance movements all brought out the political artists in quiltmakers. Today's issues, such as the hostage crisis, ecological concerns, and the homeless, have motivated modern quilters.

See also: Cause quilts

PATTERNS

The names and variations of quilt patterns are too numerous to deal with in any but a very large book. There are three now in print that deal exclusively with patterns. Of these, two are devoted entirely to pieced patterns and one to both pieced and appliqué. There is a good reason for this disparity, namely that the geometric limits of pieced designs make them less subject to minute changes. Every appliqué artist redraws the rose, dogwood, or whatever design is being made, but pieced patterns usually work so well as they are that they remain much the same — with minor variations — over the years.

There are certain categories of patterns mentioned elsewhere under separate headings: stars, one-patch, four-patch, and nine-patch. Many patterns have at least two names, often in different parts of the country. The inventiveness of the names is a wonderful folk art in itself: Bear's Paw (also known as Duck's Foot in the Mud), Ocean Waves, Hole in the Barn Door, Turkey Tracks (also known as Wandering Foot), Kitty Corner, Lady-of-the-Lake, Shoo Fly, and many, many more. Many patterns symbolize specific areas: Mariner's Compass is especially popular in New England, and Sunflower in Kansas, for example. Each state has several patterns named for it. Kansas has more than most: Kansas Dugout, Rocky Road to Kansas, and Kansas Troubles are all familiar quilts.

The first pieced block designs are those seen in the borders of English medallion quilts. They are, in general, the simplest star, four-patch, and windmill designs. Such block patterns are easily created with folded

Crossed Canoes from the 1890 Ladies' Art Company pattern. Collection of Mary Barton of Iowa

and creased squares of paper, a time-honored method still in use today.

American quilters expanded the scant repertoire of block patterns inherited from the English and gave the designs exciting and truly American names, such as: Savannah Star, Fifty-four Forty or Fight, and Kansas Troubles. When the pattern companies became active at the end of the nineteenth century, the numbers and names multiplied rapidly. The newest trend in design now is toward methods, such as Georgia Bonesteel's flexicurve and Joyce Schlotzhauer's curved two-patch.

See also: Designers, Four-patch designs, Nine-patch designs, One-patch designs, Pattern companies, Star designs

PATTERN COMPANIES

Quilt patterns, instructions, and advice were published in various periodicals, notably

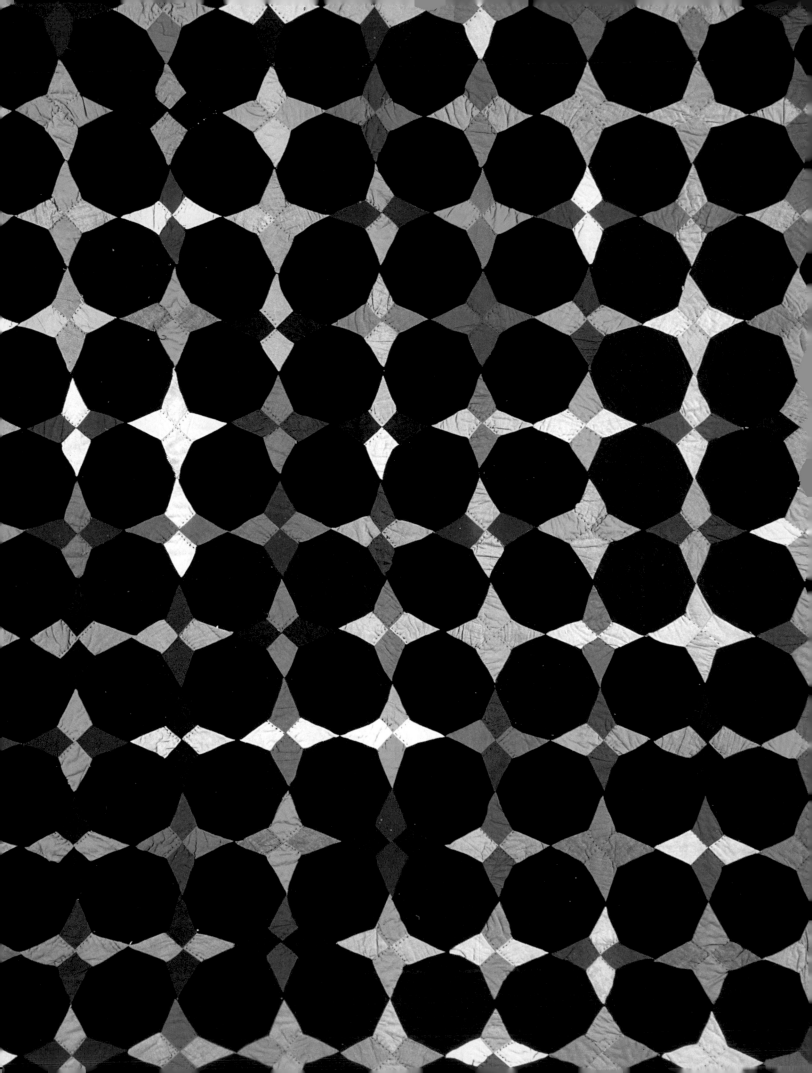

Godey's Lady's Book, in the nineteenth century. Not until 1889 did a true quilt-pattern company appear — the Ladies' Art Company of St. Louis. It was at first a family affair, run from the home. In the approximately eighty years of its existence, dozens of other companies came and went.

Pattern companies were often outgrowths of other needlework or printing companies. At about the turn of the century Frank's Art Needlework Patterns evolved from an established needlework store. The women's names by which the lines of patterns were known were often fictitious and used by companies that had other branches or services. Old Chelsea Station Needlecraft in New York published its quilt patterns under the names Alice Brooks and Laura Wheeler. Nancy Cabot was the name of patterns seen only in the Chicago *Tribune*. Colonial Patterns in Kansas City still publishes quilt patterns from Aunt Martha.

Names of real women were also given to lines of patterns. Mrs. Danner was one of the best-known of these. Ruby McKim patterns were designed by an actual woman who ran the Ruby McKim Design Studio. Both of these women can be considered pioneers of a trend that still survives among today's pattern publishers.

Stearns and Foster made batting under the trade name Mountain Mist. They and their competitor, Lockport, Rock River Cotton Company, both produced their own lines of patterns. The Lockport Company no longer exists, and their patterns can only be found in antique collections. Mountain Mist patterns used to be printed inside each roll of batting. They are now reprinted, packaged separately, and sold at a higher

price, more in line with today's market. A catalogue of all 129 of the original patterns is available. They are very complete, with finished size, quilting designs, and instructions. They cover a full range of designs, from basic pieced patterns to elaborate appliqué and quilted whole-cloth.

Many of the new pattern companies are small and have grown out of one woman's design capabilities and ingenuity. Some, like Ruth Scheel's Laughing Goose Company, print and distribute their own original designs. Others, notably the Betty Boyink Publishing Company, started with one book of fairly traditional patterns, well drafted and well presented. The owner, Betty

OPPOSITE PAGE: Many traditional pieced block patterns have more than one name. This one, from the Indiana Amish, ca. 1925, is called Hummingbird and also Periwinkle. 88 x 66". Collection of the Museum of American Folk Art, New York. Gift of David Pottinger. (Detail)

ABOVE: Floral Fantasy is typical of the appliqué quilts from one of the newest pattern companies, Quilter's Haven. It was designed by Mildred Locke in the manner of the Rose Kretsinger appliqués.

LEFT: **Oddfellow's Block with quilted wreath, made by Ann Neiswanger Lindsay of Somerset County, Pennsylvania, late nineteenth century. There are several similar patterns, such as Railroad Crossing and Flight of Geese, which appeared from every pattern company. 98 x 92". Gift of Ella B. Chapman to the D.A.R. Museum, Washington, D.C., 50.43. (Detail)**

RIGHT: **A Laura Wheeler pattern, all on one sheet of paper, with diagrams, full-size pattern pieces, and instructions. Private collection**

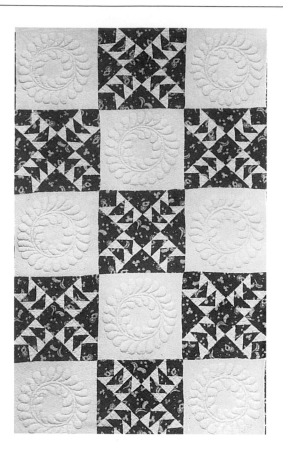

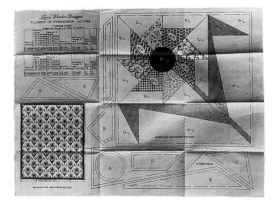

A number of peace quilts and peace banners have been made in recent years to call attention to world peace. This one is from The Ribbon: A Celebration of Life. 14 x 28"

Boyink, continues to publish at least one book of quite basic patterns and ideas each year. Mildred Locke started her line of Quilter's Haven patterns to fill a vacuum left by the disappearance of such designers as Rose Kretsinger, whose beautiful and elaborate appliqué designs were such a prominent part of the 1920-1930 period.

Today's pattern companies already rival the earlier ones for good design, and today's technology makes it possible to produce a better and more accurate product.
See also: Companies, Designers, Newspaper patterns, Periodicals

PEACE QUILTS

Women are always drawn to the cause of peace and have many times made statements for peace through quilts. During the last years of the Cold War, a group calling themselves the Boise Peace Quilters made a number of quilts to be sent to women in Russia. With these quilts they lobbied successfully to establish a dialogue with Russian women and even to go to Russia to meet them. This and The Peace Banner have been noticeably effective tools for getting the word out through newspapers and magazines that found the effort and the quilts interesting enough to cover.
See also: Banners, Cause quilts, Political quilts, Protest quilts

PERIODICALS

For over a hundred years, from the time *Godey's Lady's Book* appeared in 1830 until past the middle of the twentieth century, quilters and other needleworkers could find excellent patterns and instructions in a variety of magazines and periodicals. There were the magazines like *Home Arts Needlecraft* that specifically served these interests, but almost any general women's magazine contained pages of craft projects. In an effort to attract women readers, magazines such as *Country Gentleman* and all of the farm publications also ran quilt patterns.

Among the best-known magazine patterns are those designed by Ann Orr especially for *Good Housekeeping* and the Marie Webster patterns in *The Ladies' Home Journal*. Many of these patterns are still in use and still recognized by the designers' names. The three encyclopedias of quilt patterns now available give credit in many cases to both designer and publication.

After the middle of the twentieth century, many magazines saw an opportunity to enlarge their readership and increase the number of issues on sale by publishing special editions for needlework, knitting, and quilting. Many of these took on lives of their own, appearing as often as six times a year. *Lady's Circle Patchwork Quilts* grew out of the monthly *Lady's Circle*, having started as a once-a-year special in 1973 and expanding to six issues a year by 1984.

The current quilt revival has been the inspiration for a number of magazines devoted entirely to quilting. The first of these, and still the leader in the field, is the *Quilter's Newsletter*. It initially appeared in 1969 with only black-and-white illustrations. It is now produced in full color with ten issues a year. In 1982 its publishers added *Quiltmaker*, an attractive pattern quarterly. Other well-known and established publications are *Quilt* and *QuiltWorld*.

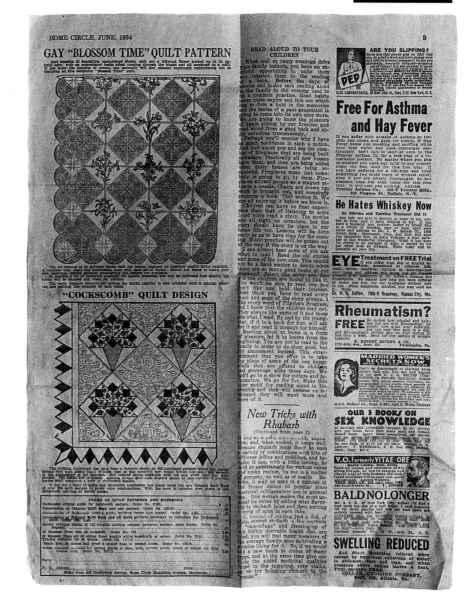

In recent years, there have been several other new publications devoted entirely to quilting, not all of them successful. The large quilting organizations and guilds also issue interesting semiannual or quarterly publications. Articles about quilting have almost disappeared from the women's service magazines except in photographs of the popular country style of decorating.
See also: Designers, Godey's Lady's Book, *Newspaper patterns, Patterns*

Typical of advertisements in periodicals of the early to midtwentieth century is this one for Colonial Quilts in the *Home Circle* magazine. Collection of Edith Rexroad

One Year's Passing by Bonita Siders of Fort Wayne, Indiana, cleverly depicts the year from spring in the upper left to winter in the lower right. 72 x 72″

PICTORIAL QUILTS

Early quilts were generally decorated with repetitive abstract designs. The Tree of Life patterns were the closest approximation of pictorial designs until American quilters began representing ships, eagles, political scenes, and so on in the early nineteenth century. These quilts were not, in the strict sense, pictorial, but they did provide the seeds of the thought that fabric could be used to create a picture.

Truly pictorial, or scenic, quilts appeared in the twentieth century, probably as late as 1920. Several existing pieces are made up of tiny squares in a sort of petit-point technique. Most are appliqué, simply following the lines of drawings. With today's intense interest in wall hangings and quilts as decorative art, scenes or abstractions of scenes are very popular.

See also: Abstract designs, Scenic motifs, Semiabstract designs

PIECED FLORALS

Flowers are charming motifs in any decorative art and especially so in quilts. They are

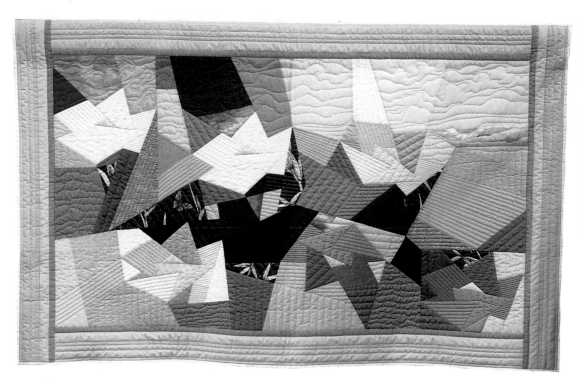

Beach Roses by Joyce Murrin of Congers, New York, is a modern abstract version of a pieced floral design. 36 x 54"

***FOLLOWING PAGE:* Pieced Sawtooth Stars in a riot of color, ca. 1870. Some quilters enjoy the intricacies of piecing and the shimmering results achieved with such tiny designs as are seen in this masterpiece. 84 x 84". Collection of Thos. K. Woodard: American Antiques & Quilts. (Detail)**

simple to reproduce in appliqué, but pieced flowers have always posed a challenge to designers. Ann Orr is famous for her floral designs worked in small squares exactly like a needlepoint graph. Other, more elaborate, versions of pieced florals appeared in various twentieth-century pattern lines. In recent years the Curved Two-Patch has allowed more flexibility in pieced floral designs. *See also: Curved Two-Patch designs, Designers*

PIECED QUILTS

"Piecing" means simply seaming together two pieces of fabric, of the same or different shapes, and continuing this process until an entire quilt top is formed. Some quilts are pieced of one shape over and over — squares, triangles, hexagons, and so on, much like the tile designs of the Near East. Other pieced quilts are made up of designed blocks, each block pieced separately, then seamed together to the desired bed size.

Several ways of joining — "setting" — the blocks may be used, further emphasizing or enhancing the designs.

Pieced quilts are the most common to America. They originated in Europe, largely in simple one-patch designs and a few block patterns, used mainly in the borders of English medallion quilts.

In the latter half of the nineteenth century, new designs began to sweep America, culminating in the formation of pattern companies such as the Ladies' Art Company in 1889. For the next sixty or seventy years quilt patterns were a staple of many newspapers, news syndicates, and magazines. Anyone with a ruler and a T-square could create new block designs.

Piecing was done by hand until the advent of the home sewing machine in the midnineteenth century. For a variety of reasons, some quilters still piece by hand — because the pieces of some designs are too

small to handle on the machine or because the quilter finds it relaxing to sew by hand. There are also new, nearly mass-production, ways of machine-piecing, especially favored by people who make quilts to sell and by those who simply want to make more quilts than time otherwise allows.
See also: Blocks, Four-patch designs, Hexagons, Mosaics, Nine-patch designs, One-patch designs, Robbing Peter to Pay Paul, Sets

PINEAPPLE DESIGNS

There are two kinds of designs known as Pineapple. One is a pieced and appliqué representation of the tropical fruit, much prized in Early America and known as the symbol of hospitality. The other is an extension of the strip-pieced Log Cabin design, an octagonal block pattern whose complexity tests the ability of quilters. It is most easily handled by the paper-piecing or press-piecing method.
See also: Foundation piecing, Log Cabin, Paper piecing, Press piecing, Strip piecing

PIPING

Skilled seamstresses have often used tiny contrasting strips of fabric, called "piping," along seams for decorative effect. These can be seen in well-made nineteenth-century quilts and are being used again today. The usual process is to fold a very fine cotton cord inside a strip of fabric cut on the bias — at a 45° angle to the straight grain. The corded bias strip is then incorporated into the seam as it is stitched. Corded piping is often used under the edge of the quilt binding as well.
See also: Binding, Seams

ABOVE: A popular arrangement of the Log Cabin Pineapple structure in the Midwest is called Windmill. This small one, made in 1920-30, is Amish. 34 x 33". Collection of the Museum of American Folk Art, New York

LEFT: Pieced and appliqué Pineapple, midnineteenth century, probably from New York State. The Pineapple was much used as a symbol of hospitality in colonial times and well into the nineteenth century. This particular quilt pattern appears in quilts from many parts of the country and Canada long before the Log Cabin Pineapple made its appearance. 77 x 74". Courtesy of The Smithsonian Institution, Washington, D.C. Gift of Miss Lenore Fallen. (Detail)

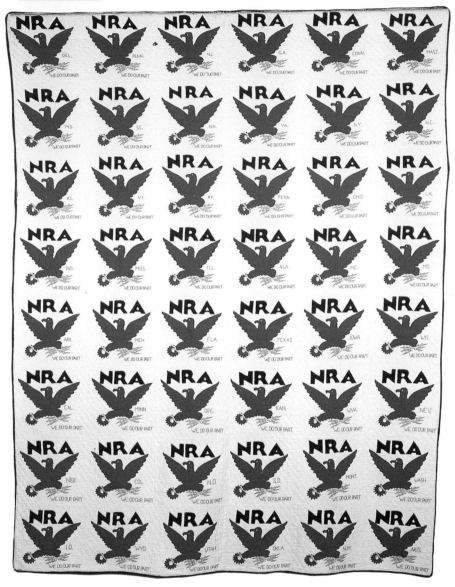

ABOVE: The National Recovery Act was a facet of Franklin D. Roosevelt's first administration that was politically popular with the masses. Ella Martin of Montcalm, West Virginia, celebrated it with its symbolic eagle and motto and with the names of the forty-eight states. Collection of the West Virginia Department of Culture and History, Charleston, West Virginia

POLITICAL QUILTS

Women have always sought to express themselves politically and have got their message across in needlework and especially in quilts. In the late nineteenth century, women championed the causes of temperance and women's rights. They backed their favorite candidates by decorating quilts with slogans and even portraits, sometimes subtly and sometimes boldly. Flags and eagles appear on the earliest American quilts, the blue and gray of the Civil War years make

allegiances unmistakable, and the Great Depression brought out quilters' support for Roosevelt's New Deal programs.
See also: Cause quilts, Memory quilts, Patriotic quilts, Temperance quilts, War quilts

POSTAGE STAMP QUILTS

One outgrowth of the twentieth-century love affair with scrap quilts and tiny piecing is the postage stamp quilt. It consists of small squares or rectangles, each no bigger than a postage stamp, made up of as many colors and fabric prints as possible. It is also a way of showing off one's skill, piecing the tiny bits into strips and then joining the strips so that seams match and the entire piece remains even.

Though some postage stamp quilts exist from around the turn of the century, they are most typical of the Depression years. The large number of prints and colors available in fabrics of the 1930s and the desire, in those hard times, to use up even the tiniest scraps made such an enterprise worthwhile.
See also: Depression quilts, One-patch designs

PRAIRIE POINTS

Folded fabric pieces called prairie points are sometimes used to make a decorative finish to a quilt's edges. The effect is similar to and sometimes confused with sawtooth edges, but they are totally different in construction. Prairie points are frequently seen on scrap quilts and other rather lighthearted country quilts.

The technique of folded pieces was used throughout the nineteenth century on the edges of jackets and on the bell sleeves of the Victorian period. Silk quilts were sometimes finished in this way with either folded fabric or ribbon. Folded points sometimes appeared on cotton quilts of the last century but began to be seen in their present form on the quilts of the 1920s. It seems perfectly in keeping with pieced patterns such as Dresden Plate and the wide assortment of bright pastels popular at that time.

See also: Edging, Sawtooth

PRESENTATION QUILTS

An old and time-honored social custom is the presentation by the community of a special and often highly personal gift to a retiring teacher, pastor, or mayor. Since at least as early as the first half of the nineteenth century, quilts have been chosen for such a gift. An entire group might make an album or signature quilt for presentation. In other cases one talented needlewoman may make the quilt to the specifications of the group. Many presentation quilts are found in museum collections because they are usually valued highly and kept in fine condition. They also frequently record some interesting facet of local history.

See also: Album quilts, Friendship quilts, Group quilts, Signature quilts

PRESS PIECING

As silks became plentiful and relatively cheap in the latter part of the nineteenth century, Log Cabin and Pineapple became very popular designs for quilts. The narrow strips of soft, slippery materials could be most easily handled by laying the center square down on a block of thin muslin or paper. Each strip was then laid right side down to the center piece, with the raw edges matching, and the seam was stitched through both layers of silk and the base, or foundation. The strip was then turned over and pressed so that it, too, was right side up and the next strip was stitched in turn, around and around until the base, or foundation, was covered. Muslin was left in, but paper was supposed to be torn out, though quilts of that period are sometimes found with the paper still in, and the back covered with a lining or backing. Often no batting was used. Log Cabin quilts are usually pieced by conventional methods today,

OPPOSITE PAGE, RIGHT: Detail of the postage stamp quilt made by Julia Adams of Maine in 1977. Each piece is about 5/8 x 3/4". The entire quilt contains 18,716 pieces

LEFT: Close-up of a corner section of prairie point edge, showing back and front, made by Barbara Dean of Virginia in 1989

though Pineapple quilts are often press-pieced on paper to keep the many strips even and the blocks square.

See also: Foundation piecing, Log Cabin, Paper piecing, Pineapples, Strip piecing

PRINTED FABRICS

Though printed fabrics were known in the countries of the eastern Mediterranean and in India before the birth of Christ, they were not common in Europe. Wool does not lend itself to printing, so linen and, later, silk were the only fabrics that could be decorated in this way until cotton was imported in quantity in the seventeenth century.

For the purpose of the study of quilts, the first important printed and painted cottons were the chintzes and the palampores of the late eighteenth century. Calico originated in Calicut in India, and became the fabric of choice for quilters from the midnineteenth century until today. The term referred first to a specific weave and later to the small prints decorating it. Today's wide choice of printed cottons offers the quilt designer a rich and interesting palette.

See also: Block printing, Calico, Chintz, Copperplate printing, Roller printing

PRIZEWINNING QUILTS

To describe a quilt as "prizewinning" should mean that it has actually won a prize in a judged show or contest. There are quilts that have gone the rounds of a dozen or so respected shows and won prizes at all of them. They are then generally retired from competition, but the maker of such quilts usually creates at least one more for the next year's shows and becomes known as the per-son to beat. The quality of workmanship of such quilters is easily recognizable even to the casual quilt-show visitor.

See also: Blue-ribbon quilts, Contests, Judged shows, Shows

PROFESSIONAL QUILTMAKING

At least as early as the seventeenth century, the textile trades in England included quilting. Bed quilts were luxury items, and quilted garments were the height of fashion in this period. In the North of England and in Wales production of the all-white whole-cloth quilts was a cottage industry in the nineteenth century and was encouraged by the government as late as the early twentieth century.

In America the actual quilting was and still is sometimes done professionally on quilts that were first pieced or appliquéd by nonprofessionals. There have also been professional markers who transferred the designs to be quilted onto the fabric. Though some quilters have made a limited living from the production of quilts for sale, it cannot be said to be a profession attracting many participants.

There have always been quilt designers in the twentieth century who are competent professionals. A number of the best quilters today are also designers, writers in the field, and teachers, making their living in much the way of other professional artists. *The Professional Quilter* magazine is published by Jeannie Spears of Oliver Press to meet their specific needs.

See also: Designers, Marking, Quilting, Teachers, Writers

The center block of this album quilt states that it was made for the Rev. and Mrs. Waterbury and presented on April 1, 1853. Many blocks have Biblical or religious significance. The origin is New Jersey. 95 x 84". Collection of the American Museum in Britain, Claverton Manor, Bath, England. Gift of Mrs. Hassel Smith

Ann Oliver made her prize-winning Painted Metal Ceilings in 1988. Since then it has been a consistant winner because of its original design, perfect appliqué, intricate quilting, and precise binding. 80 x 80"

PROTEST QUILTS

One could differentiate between cause quilts and protest quilts by noting that while there is a certain immediacy to protests, causes are more long-running. The point of a protest quilt is to bring attention to a wrong that should be righted *now*. Many women have felt more comfortable with the medium of a quilt than with speaking or writing to achieve the same purposes.

See also: Cause quilts, Peace quilts, Political quilts, Temperance quilts

PUTTING IN

Any quilter knows what another quilter means when she says her quilt is ready for "putting in." She means the top is complete and the next step is to put it in the frame with the backing and batting and start quilting. This represents an important milestone in the completion of the piece of work.

See also: Backings, Batting, Frames, Tops

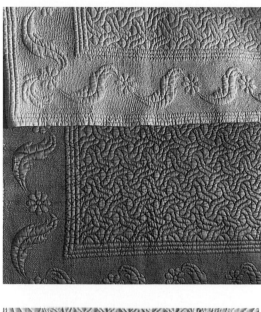

no means the only quilts made in Quaker households but they are the most recognizable. *See also: Silk*

Quilt-As-You-Go

Block-by-block quilting and quilt-as-you-go are identical techniques for finishing a quilt in sections.

See also: Block-by-block, Lap quilting

Quilting

A true, three-layered quilt is held together by a running stitch, referred to as "quilting." People speak of a "quilting stitch," but it is exactly the same in-and-out running stitch that has been used throughout history to hold the seams of garments together. Quilting, however, is more difficult and perhaps more of an art than straight sewing

ABOVE, LEFT: **Front and back of a whole-cloth, silk bed-cover, probably early nine-teenth century. The densely quilted sections show English backstitch quilting. Collection of the Stuhr Museum, Grand Island, Nebraska**

ABOVE, RIGHT: **Quaker silk quilt, midnineteenth century. 66 x 66". Collection of Susan Parrish, Antiques**

LEFT: **Typical Welsh quilting in a piece called Variations on a Welsh Theme, made by Arnold Savage using designs from *Traditional Quiltmakers* by Mavis Fitzrandolph. (Detail)**

 **Quaker Quilts**
The quilts made by the nineteenth-century Quakers were, like every-thing else they had, of very good quality, but conservative. Their clothing was always of excellent fabrics — often silk — in muted colors, and so were their quilts. One type of quilt thought of especially as Quaker is a square silk quilt pieced in a rather large design and expertly quilted. These were by

Possibly the most common background quilting designs are the Diagonal Crosshatch and the Fan. Joe Cunningham and Gwen Marston have used them here in a very sophisticated quilt, Io's Dream from their Zeus series. Zeus can be seen as a bull. 45 x 35"

with a running stitch. The difficulty lies in making the stitches small enough to carry out a design of straight or curved lines, often at a difficult angle for the quilter.

Some quilters, especially in England, use a backstitch for quilting. Presumably this makes the quilt sturdier and longer-wearing. In very old quilts the ordinary running stitch has worn well so there seems no need for elaboration.

See also: Quilting patterns, Tied quilts

QUILTING BEES

Meetings of quilters for the purpose of working on a quilt together, usually quilting a piece that has been otherwise completed, are called "bees" or "quilting bees." They have also been called "quiltings."
See also: Bees

QUILTING PATTERNS

Quilting is functional — it holds the layers of the quilt together — but it should also be decorative. The patterns used for the background should be chosen to enhance the piecing or appliqué. In the case of all-white or whole-cloth quilts several patterns can be combined to create an entire surface treatment. The overall design is usually made up of center, background, and border designs.

Some designs must have come into use because they could be traced around handy household items. One of the best-known of these is the Lemon Peel, or Wine Glass shape, which can fill an entire area with graceful interlocking circles. The circumference of a glass, and especially a wine glass, is perfect for the template. The Clamshell design, which is used for piecing, is also used for background quilting and can also be drawn around a glass. Many of the other background designs are straight-line, one of the favorites being the diagonal cross-hatch.

Many country quilts are covered with graceful curves in a pattern called Fan, or Elbow, quilting. The curves are easily drawn with a pencil tied to a string and anchored at varying lengths. It is also said that some women can draw these curves with a swing of the arm, pivoting on the elbow.

Center and block quilting designs can be taken from appliqué — bunches of flowers or hearts or wreaths. Favorite border designs are Feathers and Cables. There are stencils for these that can be moved along so that the design connects continuously. Several books of quilting patterns, as well as commercial stencils, are now available.
See also: All-white quilts, Marking, Quilting, Stencils, Whole-cloth quilts

QUILTMAKERS (NINETEENTH CENTURY)

The quiltmakers of the nineteenth century were both skilled and prolific but, alas, too few of them signed their work. Today it is the fortunate collector who can find a name on a quilt from any period, while it is almost impossible to trace the origins of many quilts over fifty years old, with or without a name. The state quilt search projects are slowly helping to remedy this situation, and more names are being recorded.

Rare are the quiltmakers, such as Mary Totten of Tottenville, Staten Island, who left records and signatures that enable us to identify quilts from the early nineteenth century. At least one of hers remains in Staten Island as part of the Richmondtown Restoration collection. Mary Evans Ford of Baltimore must have made or designed at least some of the numerous quilts attributed to her. She is generally credited with being the driving force behind the many magnificent Baltimore album quilts. Susan McCord of Indiana was an inventive quiltmaker in the last half of the nineteenth century. She also farmed and practiced herbal medicine. Not only a fine collection of her quilts, but photographs and other records of her busy life, are in the Henry Ford Museum and

Greenfield Village in Michigan. Harriet Powers was a freed slave who made story quilts based on Biblical themes, one of which is in the Smithsonian Institution and another in the Museum of Fine Arts, Boston. These few quiltmakers have become almost legendary to today's quilters. Only a handful of others are known by name.

See also: Quiltmakers (early twentieth century), Quiltmakers (late twentieth century)

QUILTMAKERS (EARLY TWENTIETH CENTURY)

Many of the well-known quiltmakers of the early twentieth century were people who were also designers and writers or historians. Marie Webster was all of these things and an innovator and trendsetter in design. Rose Kretsinger and Florence Peto also fall into this category, and examples of their writing and their quiltmaking exist today. Bertha Stenge consistently won large prizes in quilt contests of the 1930s. Dr. Jeannette Dean Throckmorton worked not only from well-known patterns such as the Mountain Mist floral appliqués but also from kits. She did all of her own quilting — not a common practice among many of the quiltmakers of the period from 1920 to 1940. She produced a large number of quilts in her lifetime, some of which can be seen in the Art Institute of Chicago. Grace Snyder of Nebraska made unusual quilts, often with thousands of tiny pieces. They have been shown by her daughter in recent years and are familiar to many quilters today. Charlotte Jane Whitehill's quilts are well known as a major part of the Denver Art Museum's collection.

See also: Quiltmakers (nineteenth century), Quiltmakers (late twentieth century)

QUILTMAKERS (LATE TWENTIETH CENTURY)

It is almost impossible to describe a cross-section of today's quilters in a way that shows the difference between this current quilt revival and anything that has gone before. There are a few highly skilled traditional quilters whose work spans this century. One of the best-known of these is Mary Schafer of Michigan, whose work inspired many new quilters in the 1970s, including Joe Cunningham and Gwen Marston.

Other essentially traditional quiltmakers who have produced an enormous number of quilts in different techniques and become known for the excellence of their work are Sally Wolff of Florida and Bernice Enyeart of Indiana. There are quilters like Martha Skelton of Mississippi who have not only made a closetful of beautiful traditional quilts but have taught many others the time-honored values of quilting.

The new wave of art quilters are individuals, each of whom has developed a style of her own, often as recognizable as any painter's. They are commissioned to create new pieces to be hung in schools and corpo-

OPPOSITE PAGE: One of several Star of Bethlehem quilts, made by Mary Totten of Tottenville, Staten Island, New York. It was made for the marriage of her niece — the names and date, "John and Mary Ann Dubois, October 6, 1835," are carefully embroidered in the lower blocks. The bias vine is little more than one eighth inch wide. 81 x 90". Collection of the Staten Island Historical Society, Richmondtown Restoration, Staten Island, New York

LEFT: Grace McCance Snyder of North Platte, Nebraska, designed many of the quilts she made, including Flower Basket Petit Point — a detail shown here. There are thirteen blocks like this, filler triangles for the edge, and a border, all pieced in tiny squares and triangles — just over one quarter inch each — for a total of nearly ninety thousand pieces in a full-size quilt. The design was suggested by a china pattern and made in 1945. 94 x 93"

Florence Peto, 1881-1970, was not only an important quilt collector but also made quilts, usually of antique fabric. In a crib quilt she preserved a selection of nineteenth- and twentieth-century patterns in nineteenth-century fabrics. 45 x 54″. Collection of the Henry Ford Museum & Greenfield Village, Dearborn, Michigan

rate offices. Among these are Nancy Halpern, Michael James, Ruth McDowell, Nancy Crow, and Judy Dales. Chris Wolf Edmonds had an art background when she turned to quilting at the time of the Bicentennial. Her work and her classes are in demand across the country. Judi Warren may have been the first person to get her M.F.A. in quilting.

The trend is for these well-known quilt artists to make themselves and their work known worldwide, to travel to Europe and

Japan and "down under" to teach their methods. Publications spread the new ideas about quilting, and the American International Quilt Association forges links between quilters. Names from England, Japan, and Australia are now becoming well known in America.

Quilting seems to be an art form whose time has finally come. When the city of Lansing, Michigan, wanted murals for the new Lansing Center, they went to a young local quilt artist named Jaquelyn Faulkner, who produced some very impressive pieces for the huge walls. The new trends do not seem to detract from the traditional strengths among quilters.
See also: Quiltmakers (nineteenth century), Quiltmakers (early twentieth century)

RAFFLE QUILTS

A time-honored way for women to make money for a favorite charity is by raffling handmade items. Quilts have always been high on the list of products with wide general appeal. A church group or quilt guild usually makes a fine quilt as a team project, one member designing the piece and several working on it. Chances are then sold, at moderate prices so as to attract more buyers and more excitement.

Once in a while a raffle quilt is commissioned by a group and made by one or two people. The money taken in must be enough to cover the commission and still benefit the charity. Some of the finest quilts today are raffle quilts, at least one of which can be found at most shows.
See also: Group quilts

RED CROSS QUILTS

In the burst of patriotic enthusiasm that marked 1917–1918, women made Red Cross quilts, as fund-raisers or as warm covers for soldiers and anyone to whom the Red Cross gave comfort. Many are similar to other fund-raisers in that they have blocks made by and the signatures of many individuals. Some are red and white, and a large number of quilts have a Red Cross design.
See also: Fund-raiser quilts, Signature quilts, War quilts

Sunburst by Rebecca Scattergood Savery, a Quaker of Philadelphia, 1770-1855. Mimi Sherman, as a result of a project started in a textile class at MAFA's Folk Art Institute, has done extensive research into the Scattergood family and their quilts, see *The Clarion*, spring 1989, vol. 14, no. 2. 118 x 125". Collection of the Museum of American Folk Art, New York. Gift of C. and M. O'Neil

RELIGIOUS QUILTS

Aside from the quilts that illustrate Bible stories, there are many other quilts with religious and moral themes. Some have verses or sayings in either pieced or appliqué letters. They are almost certainly designed by the makers and created with endless loving labor, probably in many cases for a young person going out into the world for the first time and presumably needing this moral encouragement.

See also: Bible-inspired patterns, Bible quilts

REPAIR

If a quilt is an heirloom or a treasured antique, repairs must be made very professionally. There are a number of conservators who work with all textiles, and a few who are especially interested in quilts. A museum with a good textile collection usually has information and recommendations. Some museums have certain days and hours in which they will, for a small fee, examine quilts and make suggestions about repair, cleaning, and storage. Some quilt shows recently have had conservation and repair displays. It is possible to find out from such a display what should and should not be done to a quilt.

There are a few standard rules about repair. Never add new fabric to an old quilt. Antique shops and merchant malls at quilt shows have bits and pieces of old quilts that were never completed. They are a great source of fabric for repairing other old quilts. If a delicate cotton or silk quilt is breaking up so that little pieces of fabric fall off each time it is touched, it is time to cover areas or the whole quilt with crepeline, a fine sheer silk in neutral shades. Again, a museum is the best source of information. *See also: Conservation, Crepeline*

RESEARCHERS AND HISTORIANS

Very little of women's history has been written down, but researchers have come to realize how much can be found in the quilts they made. Perhaps if a graph were drawn, it would become evident that in each phase of the women's movement quilts have taken on a significance that they were not accorded before. The first serious writing about old quilts and their historical background came after World War I, with women's suffrage and the liberated flapper era.

Florence Peto, Ruth Finley, Carrie Hall and Rose Kretsinger, and Dr. William Dunton all researched, collected, and wrote about quilts, their origins and makers. Betty Harriman researched the old designs and set about making new quilts from as many of them as possible. After she died, her friend Mary Schafer continued this work.

After World War II and through the next two decades, quilts were almost a dead issue. The Bicentennial certainly fired the new interest in them, but it seems likely that the women's movement of those years made those dim histories — a signature here, a piece of paper pinned to the back of a quilt there — seem suddenly important. Quilters and researchers into women's history began to go into the musty back rooms of museums and look at the quilts, record the scant information, and ask to have the quilts put out on display.

Cuesta Benberry in St. Louis, Joyce Gross and Sally Garoutte in California, Mary Barton in Iowa, and Barbara Bannister in Michigan collected every old pattern, every photograph, every book on quilts that they could find. At first it was fairly easy because almost no one else wanted them. Out of their interests and efforts grew the American Quilt Study Group, now headquartered in San Francisco. This organization is the foremost quilt and textile research group, and its membership includes the people who have contributed the most to today's expanding body of information on quilts. Their annual publication, *Uncoverings*, has for the past ten years added not only to knowledge about textiles but to the history of women.

It would be impossible to name all the people who have contributed to our growing knowledge of quilts and their makers, but there are some who stand out as pioneers, including all of those who have worked hard on the state quilt projects. The names of Laurel Horton, Barbara Brackman, and Katy Christopherson were among the first that were heard when quilt research became important to museums and universities.

RESIST-DYE BLUE PRINTS

Blue or indigo prints made by an elaborate resist-dye method are among the most highly prized furnishing fabrics found in Early American quilts and draperies. The designs are usually large floral repeats, sometimes extremely intricate in shading and detail. The fabric is generally a soft linen or cotton, probably homespun. There are a number of examples in American museums, but nowhere else in the world. Though they are known to be from the late eighteenth and early nineteenth centuries, there is no clear record of where or exactly how the printing was done.

The technique of resist-dyeing was known in the East for centuries before it traveled to the western world. The part of the fabric that is to remain undyed is coated with a thick wax substance applied either by painting or block-printing on the cloth, and the fabric is then put in the dye bath, permitting the uncoated parts to absorb the color. This process can be very simple or can reach sophisticated levels in which deeper shades or other colors are produced by further coating and dipping. Today's East Indian batik is quite different from the extremely complex Early American resist-dye blue fabrics that continue to mystify experts — but some conjecture that they,

LEFT: The Mariner's Compass is usually a pieced design. This one, called Compass in Reverse, by Phyllis Funk, is beautifully worked in reverse appliqué. 24 x 24″

RIGHT: Blue resist-dyed cotton from a quilted counterpane by Clara Harrison, Middlebury, Connecticut, late eighteenth century. Courtesy of The Smithsonian Institution, Washington, D.C.

Among museum curators, the names of Doris Bowman of the Smithsonian Institution and Gloria Seaman Allen of the D.A.R. Museum are highly respected. Patsy and Myron Orlofsky wrote *Quilts in America* in 1974, a book so vastly informative and accurately researched that it is still in demand by any serious student of quilts although some of its information is dated. Penny McMorris was an early researcher and writer on the artistic aspects of quilts. She hosted the first television series about them, helping to spread the knowledge of quilts as an art form throughout the public-television audience in 1981–82. Due to all of these paths of research, the interest in and preservation and knowledge of quilts continues and widens. *See also: State quilt projects, Writers*

too, came by the trade routes from the East.
*See also: Block printing, Copperplate printing,
Discharge printing, Dyes*

REVERSE APPLIQUÉ

Some appliqué designs call for a bit of color
to show through from beneath a larger
piece. This can best be achieved by cutting
a hole of the desired shape — a leaf perhaps
— in the surface piece, then turning and
stitching the edge. This is the simplest form
of reverse appliqué.

Some of the elaborate two- or three-tone
designs worked by the Hmong people are
made by laying one entire piece of fabric on
top of another, then cutting away and finishing in such a way that the under-fabric
shows through. The molas made by the
Indians of the San Blas Islands are an even
more intricate form of many-colored
reverse appliqué.

*See also: Appliqué, Hawaiian quilts, Hmong
needlework, Molas*

ROBBING PETER TO
PAY PAUL

There are a number of old and quite basic
patterns in which two simple shapes are
used in positive and negative color combinations to form more elaborate designs.
These are generally known as Robbing
Peter to Pay Paul designs. Though they are
frequently worked in only two colors, they
can be made with scraps, continuously
reversing the darker and lighter values.

The best-known among these patterns
are Dolly Madison's Workbox (also known
simply as Robbing Peter to Pay Paul),
Lafayette Orange Peel, Drunkard's Path,
Tea Leaf, Snowball, and Melon Patch. With

ABOVE: The Drunkard's Path
pieces in a more elaborate
variation, made by Julia
Needham of Tennessee in
1980. Though a larger variety of colors are used than
in the more traditional
Robbing Peter to Pay Paul
arrangement, the effect is
still achieved by interchang-
ing the lights and darks.
72 x 86". Private collection.
(Detail)

LEFT: Drunkard's Path,
detail of the quilt shown on
page 166. The two shapes
that form the entire pattern
are alternated in light and
dark to form the intricate
Robbing Peter to Pay Paul
design. Private collection

the exception of the references to Dolly
Madison and Lafayette, the names denote
the rather uncomplicated origins of these
patterns, which become intricate only by
virtue of the interchange of colors. The
Drunkard's Path is the most interesting, in
that by using up to thirty-six of the small,
two-part squares that make up the entire
pattern, alternating light and dark and turn-

An all-time favorite Rose design is sometimes called Whig Rose and sometimes Democrat Rose. The five large blocks are typical of quilts of the late nineteenth century — this one made in 1860-70 by Ruth Ann Stottlemeyer of Platt County, Illinois. 87 x 87″. Courtesy of The Smithsonian Institution, Washington, D.C. Gift of Miss Margaret A. R. Stottlemeyer, sister of the maker

ing the squares, several dozen designs can be formed.

Recently, a new pattern of this type has come into being, with seemingly limitless design possibilities. It is known as the curved two-patch and should not be confused with Drunkard's Path.
See also: Curved two-patch designs

ROLLER PRINTING

The great breakthrough in fabric printing in the late eighteenth century was the roller, which quickly put commercial block-printing out of business. The roller presses of today work on the same principles as the one patented by Thomas Bell in 1783, though with more speed and better color capability. All of the millions of yards of print fabric used by decorators and quilters

would not have been possible to manufacture by any other method.
See also: Block printing, Calico

ROSE MOTIFS

Flowers are the predominant subject of appliqué quilts, and of all flowers roses are certainly the most popular. They are more difficult to design and to handle than tulips but the possibilities for graceful design arrangements are greater. Some appliqué roses are quite realistic-looking, but many are made on the plan of a scalloped circle around another scalloped circle, called Rose of Sharon. Among the great nineteenth-century appliqué quilts there are many rose designs obviously drafted by the quilters — very beautiful pieces of textile art.

The Whig Rose, an especially elaborate pattern, appeared around the middle of the nineteenth century, just in time for the last gasp of the Whig political party. The twentieth century brought two types of pieced roses, Ann Orr's petit-point designs in tiny squares and Joyce Schlotzhauer's curved two-patch designs. In recent years appliqué roses have again been popular, especially for group sampler quilts, possibly because there are so many patterns now available.
See also: Appliqué, Curved Two-Patch designs, Floral motifs, Pieced florals, Sampler quilts

RUFFLES

Very few quilts are finished with ruffles, but in the Victorian period, with its excess of everything, both fabric and lace ruffles were popular, even on quilts. Today they are reserved mostly for baby quilts and decorator quilts for very feminine bedrooms.
See also: Edging, Lace

SAMPLER QUILTS

There seem to be two especially popular types of sampler quilts, that is, quilts with a number of different block designs arranged to blend together. One is the familiar learning sampler, a series of blocks that a teacher chooses for their specific learning values. The student chooses a group of fabrics that can be used for all of the blocks, thereby making it less difficult to set them together harmoniously. They are usually set together with sashes so that a dozen or so blocks can be extended into a quilt large enough for a bed.

The other sampler quilts are often made by groups, all of whose blocks are unified by one theme. These can be created for a special-occasion quilt like the Bicentennial ones, or the blocks can be related by pattern type. Rose samplers are very popular because there are so many beautiful rose designs available. Star-block patterns are another favorite for group samplers. There have been at least two books written on the subject of planning group samplers. These are often used as fund-raisers or presentation quilts.

See also: Bicentennial quilts, Fund-raiser quilts, Presentation quilts, Star designs

SASHES

One common way of joining blocks together to make a quilt top is to use sashes — strips of fabric — making a lattice effect between the blocks. The sashes may be quite plain or elaborately decorative. They may incorporate appliqué or quilted designs in keeping with the block design, or they may be heavily quilted. Sashes may be con-

tinuous or else have corner blocks, thereby contributing yet another element to the total design.

See also: Blocks, Corner blocks

SASHIKO

In Japan in past centuries, while the upper classes wore elegant, embellished silks, the peasants wore cotton, mostly woven at home, as coarse fabrics were in any other part of the world. Because Japan's winters are cold it was necessary to put together layers of rough cotton for the pants, jackets, and kimonos the peasants wore. These layers were held together by running stitches, much like quilting. It did not take long for the Japanese, with their love of design, to start applying the stitches in regular and charming patterns to enhance the appearance of the garments. This technique,

A Rose sampler made by the members of Quilters Anonymous in Washington State. Some quilters used traditional Rose designs and some designed their own. 87 x 72″

RIGHT: *Sashiko*-quilted cotton kimono with panels of stencil-printed cotton. Japanese quilting developed into a decoration in itself as early as the Meiji period (nineteenth century), when this piece was made. Collection of Fifi White

BELOW: Basket of Flowers, ca. 1935, made by Elizabeth Schumacher of Leece, Missouri. The bravura touches of this piece, from the freestanding flowers and intricate quilting to the scalloped edges, are typical of the fine needlework of the period. 95 x 86″. Collection of the Museum of American Folk Art, New York. Gift of Marian Boer

known as *sashiko* and now practiced in Japan and America, adheres to standard patterns, usually with white thread on dark blue. It is generally decorative rather than practical. *See also: Japanese influence, Quilting*

SAWTOOTH EDGES

Not all quilts are bound on the edges, and not all edges are smooth and even. Two interesting edges are zigzag — or when it ends in sharp points all around, the sawtooth — and the prairie point. These terms are sometimes, mistakenly used interchangeably.

If a quilt is made up of small squares set diagonally, the last row will naturally form a zigzag effect, or sawtooth edge. This must be finished by turning the top and back edges in toward each other and slip stitching them together carefully and invisibly. *See also: Edging, Prairie points*

SCALLOPS

The variety of imaginative edges on quilts attests to the endless inventiveness of quilters. It also may be a way of showing off the sewing ability of the individual quilter. A neat binding on a quilt is difficult enough, but binding around scallops is very demanding. The two edges most often finished in this way are on the Double Wedding Ring quilt and the Ice Cream Cone border, popular early in the twentieth century. *See also: Binding*

SCENIC MOTIFS

The idea of "painting" a picture with fabric has long appealed to quiltmakers. Large scenic designs, especially depictions of farms and homes, seem the most popular. Though appliqué is a more workable medi-

um, many pieced or partially pieced land-scapes have also been made. The system of using tiny squares set together to resemble needlepoint charts can create quite realistic effects. Works of this type are almost always one of a kind, though there have been a few commercial patterns for smaller wall hangings.

See also: Pictorial quilts

PREVIOUS PAGE: **Heartlands by Nancy Applegate is a tribute to the fields and barns of Ohio. The scenic effects are all achieved through the mediums of piecing and quilting, no appliqué. 60 x 60"**

RIGHT: **Good scissors and cutting tools for quilting include, from left to right, appliqué scissors, cutting shears, embroidery scissors, and a roller cutter**

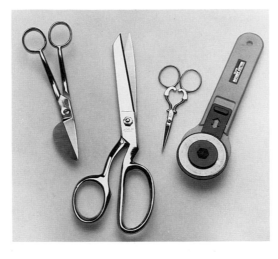

SCISSORS

Very few special scissors have been invented for quilters, with the exception of appliqué scissors, which have a protective flange on one blade to make it easier to slide the scissors along on the fabric without nicking into a layer that should not be cut. In general, the same good sharp steel scissors appropriate for any other fine sewing are right for quilting. It is also nice to have fine scissors for snipping thread.

Other cutting tools have come on the market to make quilting easier and quicker. Rotary cutters and gridded transparent plastic mats have revolutionized cutting for pieced quilts. There are very small thread snippers, safer than scissors to leave lying on the quilt top when not needed.

SCRAP QUILTS

Anyone who has sewn or made quilts will eventually amass a large collection of left-over fabric. Individual taste always surfaces in such a collection and it is easy to see how colors and fabric types relate. With a little careful designing, the random pieces can be combined to create a scrap quilt that appears to have been more or less planned.

During the Depression, many stores and mail-order sources catered to the idea of the scrap quilt, packaging scrap bundles at a nice low price. Most stores that serve quilters today sell "quilter's quarters" so that it is easy to fill in colors and prints as needed.

When the new wave of quilting started in 1976, few people had such extensive collections of fabric, so scrap quilts were not in favor. By now many of these people are dedicated quilters and have accumulated an extensive collection of small pieces suitable for making scrap quilts even more exciting than the earlier ones designed by their mothers and grandmothers.
See also: Calico, Charm, One-patch, Postage stamp

SEAMS

The most basic stitching technique is sewing a seam. There are several types of seams, but for the sake of simplicity only the plain seam that is used in quilting will be discussed here. At its simplest, a seam is a line of stitching that joins two pieces of fabric. The two pieces of fabric are laid right sides together, with the raw edges meeting. A line is then stitched parallel to the raw edge — for quilts, the distance from the edge is usually one-quarter inch. When the two pieces of fabric are pulled away from each other so that the right sides of both are seen, the line of stitching will hold them firmly together along the designated seam line.
See also: Piping

SELF-BINDING

It requires very careful examination to determine the method used to bind quilts. One system that was used more in early

Kansas Sunset by Jean V. Johnson shows that a scrap quilt need not be unplanned. She says she used a "straightened Drunkard's Path" as the basis of the design. The final appearance is a medallion as seen through a grid. 90 x 108". Courtesy of Jean V. Johnson

quilts — through the nineteenth century — than it is now was self-binding, that is, bringing the edge of the quilt backing over the top and stitching it in place. If this is done well, and the binding folded narrowly and evenly and stitched with invisible stitches, it makes a very neat finish.

See also: Binding, Edging

SEMIABSTRACT DESIGNS

Whereas abstract art depicts nothing from the world of nature or of made objects, semiabstract art hints at these forms. For example, the buildings and ships in works by the semiabstract artist Lionel Feininger are completely recognizable but highly stylized. The same trends appear in modern

quilt art. Nancy Halpern, Jaquelyn Faulkner, and Judy Dales are known for exciting semiabstract depictions of landscapes, towns, and buildings.

See also: Abstract designs, Art quilts

SEMINOLE STRIP PIECING

The sew-and-cut strip piecing known as Seminole is not normally used for quilts, but for vividly colorful clothing. It is practiced commercially by the Seminole Indian women of Florida. The fabric is usually a cotton and polyester blend, though it was once all cotton. The colors are bright, and no prints are used. There are dozens of patterns achieved by piecing long strips of fabric, cutting the strips, and joining the raw ends to form rows of diagonal blocks.

Seminole piecing is an art born of necessity and a natural artistic ability. Some form of piecing was probably taught to the Seminoles when they were moved to Florida and put on reservations. When they acquired sewing machines — probably the hand-cranked kind — around 1900, this new form of piecing was born. The results were and have continued to be of commercial value.

On one reservation in Immokalee, Florida, the women work, as their mothers and grandmothers did, in thatched, one-room houses called "chickees." The only modern improvement seems to be that electricity has been run into the workplace so that the women can use very heavy, fast sewing machines. The full skirts and colorful jackets decorated with many bright pieced strips and yards of rickrack are the standard costume of the women on the reservation, as well as their main livelihood.

See also: Indian influence (American), String piecing, Strip piecing

SETS

When quilters speak of assembling a quilt, they may refer to "sets and sashes" or they may speak of "setting" the blocks. There are a number of ways to join pieced or appliqué blocks together to make a complete top. One is described under Sashes, but there are other ways of setting the blocks without sashes.

One such set is the alternating of pieced or appliqué blocks with plain blocks. The blocks may be set square or they may be placed diagonally — sometimes referred to as "hung on the diamond." A further elaboration of this set is worked by cutting the plain blocks into two triangles and slipping the halves in such a way that they form a zigzag pattern between the decorated blocks. This is known as Streak of Lightning or, in Nova Scotia, as Herringbone.
See also: Sashes

SEWING MACHINES

From the time of the first available home sewing machine — about 1850 — to today, quilters have discussed and argued the relative merits of hand- and machine-stitching. The first known mechanical stitching device was invented around 1790, but it was not until 1846 that Elias Howe took out a patent for the true precursor of today's home sewing machine.

By 1850 women in the industrial centers of America were becoming excited by the prospect of a machine that would eliminate the long hours of hand-stitching required to make the elaborate clothing of the period. Quilters also began to think in terms of greater output in less time. It is possible to find quilts of the midnineteenth century with machine piecing, bindings stitched by machine, and even appliqué painstakingly laid on with tiny machine stitches.

In the post-1976 quilting renaissance there has been considerable discussion of the relative merits of hand- and machine-stitching on quilts. The writers of contest rules have often specified "no surface

LEFT: **Blazing Star blocks in a Streak of Lightning set, by Julia Needham of Tennessee, 1984. 75 x 88". (Detail)**

BELOW: **Guardians of Liberty by Amy Chamberlin is a combination of appliqué and "stitch painting," worked on a home sewing machine. The likenesses were taken from various postcards and books. Detail of two machine-stitched portraits. 86 x 91"**

machine stitching," meaning that only the piecing can be done by machine. As quilters have become more skilled in the use of zigzag machines and have developed ways of quilting and doing appliqué on sewing machines, the rules have changed. There are special awards in contests for machine appliqué and machine quilting. Many of the new breed of art quilts owe their unusual beauty to elaborate machine-stitching.
See also: Appliqué, Pieced quilts, Quilting

RIGHT: The gigantic Houston Quilt Festival and Market is the largest event of its kind in the United States. This picture, taken from the second floor balcony, shows only a segment of the varied shows and many booths within the 100,000-square-foot floor space of the George R. Brown Convention Center

BELOW: A museum quilt show, Pieced by Mother, in 1987, presented Pennsylvania quilts like this Jacob's Ladder by Katherine Geise Urban of North Umberland County, ca. 1910, in the Kelly Gallery of the Packwood House Museum in Lewisburg, Pennsylvania

SHIPPING

It is often necessary to ship a quilt or quilts to a show and it is very important to see that they travel safely. A few simple precautions will ensure that the quilt is not damaged.

Fold it wrong side out and put it in an old pillowcase. Slip the pillowcase and quilt into a plastic bag. Use a firm corrugated carton that gives the bagged quilt room.

Always place an address card inside the box. Tape the box closed firmly and use a typed address label outside, making sure that there is a complete return address.

There is a wide range of excellent carriers in an equally wide price range. If speed is necessary, next-day delivery is possible almost everywhere. All carriers will insure the quilt, but if it is very valuable, it is wise to have it appraised first and to show a signed appraisal.

Here are ideas on shipping, gathered from the many stories told by quilters:

Pack only one quilt in a box — in the unlikely event that one box is lost, all is not lost.

Do not write "Quilt," or anything relating to quilts on the outside of the box.

Registered mail is slower than some other methods but so safe that even jewelers use it.

See also: Appraisals

SHOWS

A nostalgic part of American tradition is the showing and judging of quilts. Small shows have always been and still are held in parish halls for the benefit of churches. The local school, grange hall, and firehouse have a long tradition of quilt shows, both judged and invitational. It is hard to think of any other art or craft that has such wide appeal and enough variety to keep the people of a community coming back each year.

Quilt shows were part of the Centennial and Bicentennial celebrations, world's fairs, and the celebration of the hundredth anniversary of the Statue of Liberty. The late twentieth century has seen quilts taken far more seriously by museums than ever before, with a number of traveling quilt shows setting records for attendance in museums across the country.

The growth of rapid transportation and the increasing number of convention spaces large enough to handle thousands of people have led to a new phenomenon — the commercial quilt show or festival. There are usually several shows within the larger show, at least one judged and another invitational. There are vending booths, lectures, and classes — all quilt-related. Leaders in this field are The Houston Festival in Texas and the Great American Quilt Show in New York.

See also: Invitational shows, Judged shows, Juried shows, State fairs

Simple signature blocks, one dated 1872, may have been made by any number of people and used as a fund-raiser or presentation quilt. Collection of the Claflin-Richards House, Wenham, Massachusetts. (Detail)

SIGNATURE QUILTS

Quilts from about the middle of the nineteenth century to the present that bear a large number of signatures, either inked or embroidered, may have been made for a variety of reasons. Many were used as fund-raisers for churches or other institutions. Some were presentation quilts for beloved ministers or other members of the community. A few appear to have been protest quilts, expressing the sentiments of a group of people involved in, for example, the temperance movement.

See also: Friendship quilts, Fund-raiser quilts, Presentation quilts, Protest quilts

SIGNING

Researchers owe a great debt of gratitude to the quiltmakers who sign their work. A signature with a date and place of origin makes it possible to trace an entire story and often to find existing members of the family.

Some quiltmakers have bravely signed the center of the quilt top. Others have embroidered their names and dates inconspicuously in a corner or on a border. In a few rare cases the name has been worked into the design as an essential element. Today the

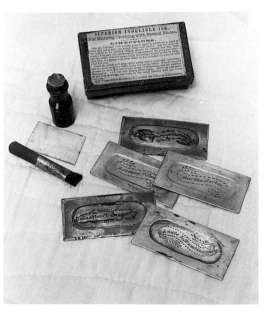

ABOVE: Emily Hobart's quilt presents no problems to future generations. It is boldly signed in appliqué, in the border. She includes her town, county, and state, the date in two places, and some of her sentiments about life. 84 x 101". Courtesy of The Smithsonian Institution, Washington, D.C. Gift of Mr. and Mrs. John Beard Ecker

RIGHT: Stencil plates, ink, and brush for marking household linens. In the midnineteenth century many quilts were marked with these ink stencils, which were sometimes used to print signatures on autograph blocks. Collection of Sara Dillow

trend is toward neatly embroidered labels sewn to the back of the quilt. In some cases such labels are inked and bear a fairly long description of when and why the quilt was made and by whom.

See also: Appraisals, Dating textiles, Researchers and historians

SILK

Silk has probably been used for quilts and quilted clothing as long as or longer than any other fabric. The fact that both silk and the technique of quilting were known in the Orient before they were introduced into Europe makes this assumption seem reasonable.

Early household records from England as long ago as the sixteenth century mention "quylts" of silk. There were also wool and linen quilts, but it is more difficult to work delicate quilted designs on these heavier fabrics. Not only bedcovers, but petticoats and other clothing for royalty and the wealthy would more often have been of the finer silk.

In the late seventeenth and early eighteenth centuries, cotton from India became readily available for precise handwork. Early American whole-cloth quilts are most often made of cotton or the heavier woolens, either glazed or unglazed.

Not until the nineteenth century was silk a fabric of choice for American quilters. In the second quarter of that century, full bed quilts were pieced of silk in much the same patterns used for pieced cottons. A few of these remain intact in museums. The Newark Museum in New Jersey has an especially fine example signed and dated "C. S. Conover, 1855." In the next quarter-century silk dress scraps were used in many

A Log Cabin Pineapple wall hanging in lightweight silks, made in the first half of the twentieth century, probably in southern Wisconsin. 80 x 80″. Collection of Kay Sorensen

smaller parlor throws. Simple designs, such as pieced stars and Log Cabins, were favored. Then the crazy quilts of the high Victorian period took over, with silk, velvet, and wool predominating.

In the late nineteenth and early twentieth centuries, some very fine silk quilts were made that can only be described as "dressmaker quilts" because, where the history of these quilts is available, it is known that the makers worked with scraps from their daily business, either in clothing factories or as ladies' dressmakers. Nowadays, silk appears mainly in so-called wearable art or art quilts. *See also: Art quilts, Clothing, Victorian crazy quilts, Wearable art, Whole-cloth quilts*

SLAVE-MADE QUILTS

Before the Civil War there were skilled slaves who worked as dressmakers and needleworkers, often along with the plantation mistress. In most cases only legend and family histories can identify the quilts made by these women. Some museums, especially

be confused with African-American quilts, which have distinct, more identifiable styles.
See also: African-American quilts, Story quilts

SLEEVES

One of the best ways to hang a quilt for display is to use a rod or pole as long as the quilt is wide. To attach the quilt to the rod, a strip of fabric of the same length is sewn to the quilt backing near the top edge, with open ends through which the rod can pass. Such a casing is usually referred to as a "sleeve." All quilts to be displayed in shows should have sleeves about three to four inches wide. They should be sewn firmly in place by hand, even catching through to the outside of the quilt at points to prevent pulling the backing.

SPREADS

The use of the word "spread" or "bedspread" to describe a cover for the bed seems to have replaced "counterpane" in the middle of the nineteenth century. An unabridged 1859 Webster dictionary defines "spread" in several ways, including "a cloth used as a cover" — no mention of beds. In the last decades of the century, spreads, including Marseilles spreads for the bed, were commonly advertised.
See also: Coverlets, Marseilles spreads

SQUARES

Quilts are often composed of squares of fabric put together to form various designs. These are commonly called "blocks."
See also: Blocks, Sets

STAR DESIGNS

If one could count all the pieced quilts and

ABOVE: An embroidered summer spread in Turkey-red thread and a style popular at the turn of the century. This piece has a backing to cover the reverse side of the embroidery, but no batting or filler. 60 x 61". Collection of the Museum of American Folk Art, New York. Gift of Dr. Robert Bishop

RIGHT: A sleeve carefully attached to the upper edge of the backing of a quilt, which was made to celebrate the 200th anniversary of the Coast Guard. The sleeve is firmly hand-sewn on both edges and open at the end for inserting a rod

in the South, have records accompanying such quilts that identify them as slave-made. In general, they can not be identified by style or type, because they were made for use in the plantation house to the specifications of the mistress or even by a slave working with the mistress. They are not to

all the patterns used for piecing and divide them meticulously into categories, the one motif that would undoubtedly predominate is the star. One reason is that star patterns, especially easy to create by folding a square of paper, demand no drawing skill. Another may be that the star is a universal and easily recognizable symbol.

Among the few block patterns that came from England to America were simple stars based on the division of a square into nine or sixteen equal squares. These still exist in

American patterns as the Variable and the Sawtooth stars. There are so many variations on these two basic shapes alone that it would be impossible to list them.

The other widely used stars are the Eight-Point Star, derived from an octagon and sometimes called Lemon Star or Star of Lemoyne, and the Six-Point, or Hexagon, Star. The Eight-Point Star can be worked in multiple rows, until, as in the Star of Bethlehem, it covers the entire bed.

The Feathered Star in its many variations is a test of piecing skill. It is usually based on the Variable Star (a nine-patch) or the Sawtooth Star (a sixteen-patch division of the four-patch). It is more rarely a variation of the octagonal Lemon Star. The one identifying feature is the fringe of small

ABOVE, LEFT: A California Star is an elaborate Feathered Star on a sawtooth base with a nine-patch center containing five variable stars. This one is probably from the late nineteenth century. Collection of James and Sandra Pape

ABOVE, RIGHT: A full-size Feathered Star sampler by Carol Doak won the best-of-show at the 1986 Vermont Quilt Festival. 86 x 86″

LEFT: Broken Star, made in 1939 in Harrogate, Tennessee, by Mary Williams Jones. This variation of a Star of Bethlehem was popular in the Depression periods as were the brilliant solid pastels and the fine quilting in the white areas. Private collection

triangles, or "feathers," around each point — the piecing of this pattern obviously requires great ability.

See also: English quilts, Four-patch designs, Hexagons, Nine-patch designs, Octagons, Raffle quilts

STATE BIRDS AND FLOWERS

Quilts reflect local concerns and local politics, making it easy to determine where many quilts originated. In the first half of the twentieth century, when there was keen competition among the pattern companies and newspapers for variety in quilt designs, state bird and state flower motifs came into being. They were embroidered in small block formats so that forty-eight of them put together made a good size quilt. Some of these motifs were available printed on muslin ready to embroider, others were hot-iron transfers, and still others had to be traced.

See also: Embroidery

STATE FAIRS

From at least as early as the midnineteenth century until today, state fairs have encour-

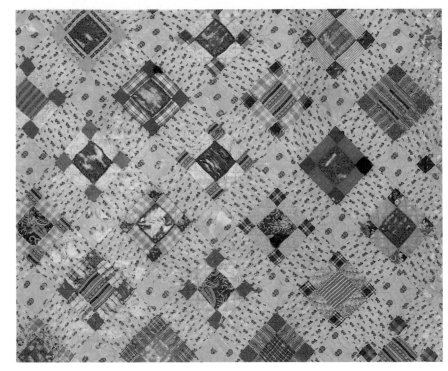

aged quilt displays and awarded prizes to the best. Even in times when quilts were not especially popular, there always seemed to be a place for them among the needlework, canning, and other home arts presented at state fairs, especially in the Midwest.

See also: Contests, Judged shows, Prizewinning quilts, Shows

STATE QUILT PROJECTS

In 1982 a group of Kentucky women headed by Katy Christopherson started an organized search for quilts made in that state. Their purpose was to photograph and list each piece, regardless of its value, and to find out as much as possible about the history of both quilts and makers. The immediate

ABOVE: The winner of the first prize in the first Minnesota State Fair, 1859, was an old-fashioned nine-patch made by Marie Marrisette. 83 x 78″. Minnesota Historical Society Museum Collections, St. Paul. Gift of Elvert F. Connolly, grandson of maker. (Detail) 69.184

Members of the Ohio Quilt
Research Project inspected,
measured, photographed,
and recorded every quilt
brought to them, creating a
permanent record of over
seven thousand quilts

Members of the Ohio Quilt
Research Project inspected,
measured, photographed,
and recorded every quilt
brought to them, creating a
permanent record of over
seven thousand quilts

result was a show of Kentucky quilts that
moved many other states to start programs
to document their quilts.

The quilt projects have been run in a
variety of ways: by guilds, with sizeable
grants, with input and help from universities and historical societies, and with growing interest and participation from communities and the nation. The publication of a
book has become almost a customary outgrowth of each quilt search. North Carolina
now has a file of over ten thousand quilts
photographed and documented. In many
cases the pictures and considerable histories
of the makers are included.

Much of the work of quilt projects is
accomplished by unpaid volunteers, whose
only interest is in seeing this art form and
the women artists accorded recognition.
Undoubtedly, one result has been to inspire
museums to take a new look at their quilt

collections, and accord them a higher prior
ity and more frequent displays.
*See also: Documentation, Identification,
Researchers and historians*

STENCILED DESIGNS

Itinerant artists in the first half of the nineteenth century had a number of skills,
including simple stenciling for the decorating of walls. The borders and panels that
they created were probably a comparatively
inexpensive alternative to wallpaper, most of
which would still have been imported. The
subjects were simple: fruit, flowers, hearts,
and the like.

The stenciling of fabrics in many of the
same designs was done nonprofessionally by
women for their own homes. The designs
were used for curtains, quilts, and coverlets.
Little, if any, fabric stenciling was done
commercially. For some reason, fabric

Stenciled summer spread, ca. 1830. Painting and stenciling on fabric were very popular in the mid-nineteenth century and a few quilts from that period survive. The art had something of a rebirth in about 1980 and is still a popular way of decorating quilts. 86 x 75″. Collection of the Museum of American Folk Art, New York. Gift of Dr. Robert Bishop

painting of any kind in America falls into the category of "women's art." There are some examples of stenciled quilts and coverlets in museum collections, but they are relatively rare.

In the post-Bicentennial quilt revival, stenciling again became popular. It is compatible with country-style decorating and is being used again on walls. Less time-consuming than appliqué, stenciled designs are especially popular for children's quilts. The market has met this new demand for stencil material with books, patterns, and better paints and brushes.

See also: Appliqué, Stencils

STENCILS

The intricate quilting designs, repeated over the surface of a quilt, are usually traced around a stencil made of metal, cardboard,

ABOVE: A story quilt made on commission by Annie Dennis in 1984 for Edna Ferguson of Natchez, Mississippi

Right Quilting stencils, made of light cardboard and firm paper, from Mennonite or Amish quilters in Indiana. Collection of Rebecca Haarer

wood, or, more recently, plastic. Stencils are also used for appliqué designs. The patterns for pieced quilts are simple geometric shapes usually referred to as templates though they are actually stencils of a sort.
See also: Patterns, Quilting, Templates

STITCHES

Beside the embroidery stitches used on Victorian crazy quilts, two stitches are the basis of all quilting. The running stitch is used for piecing (unless it is done on the sewing machine) and for quilting. It is the simplest and oldest form of sewing — pushing the needle in and out in a line. The only skill involved is keeping the stitches small and even.

The basic stitch for appliqué is a blind stitch — one that is hidden in the base fabric and catches only the tiniest fold on the edge of the applied design. In recent years this stitch has been improved by some of the excellent appliqué artists now teaching, but the purpose is still the same, an invisible but strong means of holding the applied piece in place.
See also: Appliqué, Quilting

STORY QUILTS

From prehistoric times people have told stories in pictures. Native Americans decorated pottery, hides, even their dwellings, with figures of men and animals enacting familiar legends. Textiles have been woven or their surface decorated with pictures and symbols. Appliqué is used by the Cuna-Cuna Indians on their molas and by the people of Dahomey for their story cloths.

The best-known story quilts are African-American, often depicting Biblical themes. These are usually appliqué and often appear unplanned, as if the various elements were worked at different times and in different moods.

Because terms are used loosely among quilters, any quilt that tells a story or depicts a portion of one's life can be called a "story" quilt. As more quilters design their own pat-

terns and attempt to make statements with their work, more such story quilts are being seen.

See also: African-American quilts, Pictorial quilts

STRING PIECING

In the nineteenth century, when almost all clothes were made at home, the sign of a frugal and careful dressmaker was that she had no fabric left over after cutting out a dress except long narrow strips, or strings, no more than an inch or two wide. Quilters soon saw the usefulness of these pieces and

invented block patterns like Log Cabin, in which they could use even the tiniest scraps. These organized patterns are usually called "strip" designs. True "string" quilts are made up of uneven strips pieced together on a paper or muslin back and then cut into a traditional pattern such as Stars or World Without End.

See also: Foundation piecing, Log Cabin, Paper piecing, Press piecing, Strip piecing

STRIP PIECING

The term "strip piecing" (not to be confused with "strippy" quilts) covers a variety of techniques and is used differently in different areas. Log Cabin and Pineapple designs can be described as strip-pieced. The term is also used interchangeably with

LEFT: Two Kentucky quilts in the identical pattern, made by two quilters in the same family. The startling effect of string-piecing can be seen in the red version. Private collection in Florida

ABOVE: Spider Web is a strip- or string-pieced pattern based on an octagon. Zoorett Freeman of West Virginia uses newspaper to stabilize her blocks until they are all sewn together

English-style strippy quilt, ca. 1830. The American versions of these simple quilts were often made more elaborate with the addition of borders or other design elements. Collection of Ann Kovalchick

"string piecing," though to many quilters there is some difference. The piece-and-cut method used in Seminole piecing is another strip technique.

See also: Foundation piecing, Log Cabin, Paper piecing, Pineapples, Press piecing, Seminole strip piecing, String piecing, Strippy quilts

STRIPPY QUILTS

Many quaint expressions in quilting seem to have originated in the North of England — among them "strippy" to describe a quilt made up of lengthwise bands of two different fabrics, often heavily quilted in the North of England manner. Such quilts were very popular in the late nineteenth and early twentieth centuries. They seem to have been made of one bed-length each of two

fabrics, a more decorative and probably more expensive print and a plain white or muslin. Each fabric was thirty-six or thirty-nine inches wide, so that every bit of the fabric was used to make a quilt of about seventy-two inches, the usual size for a bed.

Strippy quilts, though economical, were carefully and artistically planned. The darker color was usually used for the side and center panels and alternate ones between — making five or seven colored panels and an even number of white ones. The quilting was usually worked in a pattern that conformed to the width of the strips. Sometimes a strippy piecing is used for the back of a pieced quilt, and then the design of the quilting conforms to the top rather than to the back.

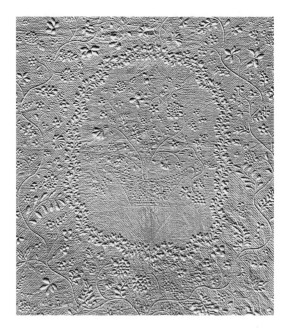

LEFT: **Early nineteeth-century stuffed-work quilt from Pennsylvania. Courtesy of America Hurrah, New York City. (Detail)**

RIGHT: **A new Sunbonnet Girl crib quilt, designed and made by Patricia Cox for her One-of-a-Kind Pattern Company. 45 x 60″**

In America, quilts were arranged in this manner but often with the darker strip pieced in a continuous design and the alternating plain strip heavily quilted. Some of these quilts are very elegant and decorative and probably served as a way to stretch very fine chintz or other treasured fabric into something more than just a scrap quilt.
See also: Strip piecing

STUFFED WORK

Whole-cloth quilts and quilts with large white areas are often embellished with quilting in which some of the motifs are heavily stuffed with batting to give a raised effect. This technique is sometimes mistakenly called "trapunto." The method is quite different (see Trapunto) and the effect less delicate.
See also: All-white quilts, Marseilles spreads, Whole-cloth quilts

SUMMER COVERLETS

When quilts were an important part of the decor of well-furnished homes, they were often replaced in warm weather with lighter coverlets, or spreads. These might be embroidered or woven but often they were identical to quilts, except that they had no batting.

In the early and midnineteenth century the popular *broderie perse* tops were often lined and not batted, and thus were suitable for summer use, while being as decorative as their winter look-alikes. Other forms of appliqué were frequently used without batting. Pieced quilts, however, needing the support of batting, are not as suitable for coverlets. After the machine-made Marseilles and other spreads appeared, fewer summer coverlets were handmade — most of the summer coverlets in existing collections were made before 1850.
See also: Coverlets, Marseilles spreads, Spreads

SUNBONNET SUE

While twentieth-century appliqué patterns still included the ornate florals of the previous century, they were joined by a new style

This Martha Washington's Wreath with a swag border is one of many prize winning quilts made by Dot Finley since 1976. Elements of the central pattern are added to the swag. 82 x 82". (Detail)

— pretty ladies and girls. These were sold by many major pattern companies under the names of Colonial Ladies, Lady in the Swing, and Sunbonnet Children. The most enduringly popular of all of these designs is Sunbonnet Sue.

Sue had her origins in the *Sunbonnet Babies* primers of the late nineteenth century, some of which are still available in reprint. She was depicted on quilts from early in the twentieth century, an industrious little girl doing the chores that all children were expected to participate in at that time. In the 1920s she was joined by an Overall Boy, who went by a variety of names, but she was and still is Sunbonnet Sue. She is now undergoing a great revival, spurred on by the Groves Publishing Company's contests and publications.

Sunbonnet Sue has also been the subject of several cartoon storybooks by Jean Ray Laury. In these stories, Sue reflects the life of today's quilters, going to quilt shows and conventions and trying to keep her house clean while she spends much of her time making quilts.

See also: Appliqué, Children's quilts, Juvenile quilts, Overall Boy

SWAG BORDERS

Certainly one of the most popular border designs in quilting is the swag. It is most often used on appliqué quilts but does sometimes appear even on simple pieced designs, with which it has no apparent relationship. It may be the ease of drafting such a design that has led to its popularity. A simple process of measuring and dividing can produce a swag to fit any quilt. Bows or other decorations can serve to join each

swag to its neighbor. Elements of the overall design of the quilt are often added.

Very early nineteenth-century quilts can be found with swag borders, and from that time until the present day they have finished quilters' finest work. Perhaps the origin can be traced to the prevalence of valances and swags in elaborate Victorian homes with four-poster beds and heavily draped windows. Swags also adorn elegant pieces of china from that period. On quilts, a swag works especially well when planned so that the border starts exactly at the edge of the mattress and falls around the sides and foot of the bed.

See also: Borders, Four-poster-bed quilts

SYMBOLS

Quilters have quite often made statements or sent messages in the designs of their quilts. Hearts — obviously a symbol of love

Lucy Kemper West of Garrard County, Kentucky, made this Pineapple and Pomegranate quilt in 1860. 77 x 74". Collection of the D.A.R. Museum, Washington, D.C. 85.06

— are found tucked into the floral arrangements of appliqué or almost hidden in quilting designs. Roses are symbols of love, purity, and happiness, while red and white stood for the houses of York and Lancaster and as the symbols of several of the United States. Tulips, much used in Pennsylvania quilts, are also symbols of love. The pineapple stands for hospitality. It is seen throughout Colonial America in wood carvings over doors and on newel posts, as well as in two forms on quilts: appliqué in the first part of the nineteenth century and the pieced Log

Cabin style later. The pomegranate stands for fruitfulness and is also a favorite Early American design.

Symbols work their way into quilting from current events and the quilters' immediate concerns. Indian symbols such as the hooked cross, various peace symbols, state flowers, and especially designed state quilt blocks all say something about the maker and her concerns.

See also: Heart motifs, Pineapples, Rose motifs, State birds and flowers

Drunkard's Path, ca. 1880, from the Van Loon family of the Albany area in New York State. Blue and white were the colors of the temperance movement. 72 x 84". Private collection

TEACHERS

No art or craft is possible without teachers to inspire and spur on the willing student. Contrary to the old saw "Those who can, do, and those who can't, teach," many of today's quilting teachers are also innovators, artists, and technicians in their own right. The quilting public, and especially those who want to learn from the best, are quick to rule out second-raters.

Because such poor records of women's endeavors and history were kept until recently, it is nearly impossible to list the instructors of the past. Today's teachers are highly visible, as they jet across the country to teach at guild meetings and quilt shows. They are featured in newspapers and magazines and have large followings. Not all of today's quilting instructors are women — names of professionals like Michael James and Jeff Gutcheon are familiar and their styles influential.

Every community has its favorite teachers, many of whom hold classes at least five days a week, yet may not be known outside of their own regions. Other teachers are booked a year or more in advance for classes and lectures nationwide or even worldwide.

Though some of the teachers listed here have also written or created original patterns, they are instantly recognized for their skill as instructors. In many communities, quilters will gladly tell a visitor that much of the work being done is a result of a series of classes by Doreen Speckmann, Jean Johnson, Jinny Beyer, or Roberta Horton. The influence of these teachers may be most evident in other people's work, though they all encourage individuality. Other names familiar at the many symposia across the country are Virginia Avery, Joe Diggs, Janet Elwin, Dixie Haywood, Chris Wolf Edmonds, Helen Kelley, Mary Coyne Penders, Jean Ray Laury, Mary Golden, Elly Sienkiewicz, Mary Ellen Hopkins, and the team of Gwen Marston and Joe Cunningham.
See also: Designers, Quiltmakers (late twentieth century), Writers

TEMPERANCE QUILTS

Among the many causes espoused by women and represented in their quilts was temperance. There is historical evidence that at least some of the blue-and-white quilts of the latter half of the nineteenth century were inspired by the temperance movement, so strong at that time. Blue and white were the colors of the movement, and certainly such designs as Drunkard's Path, when executed in those colors, indicated a commitment to this crusade for sobriety.

See also: Cause quilts

TEMPLATES

The original word was "templet," probably from the French, meaning a pattern, usually of thin wood or metal. In quilting books and manuals the later spelling "template" is used. The material must be thin and hard enough so that it can be drawn around many times without wearing away or changing shape. For many years, women have also made their own templates, even though metal or wooden ones have been available in the twentieth century. They used what came to hand: firm shirt cardboards and later the sides of large plastic milk containers. A preferred material now is a translucent stencil plastic, available at art- and quilt-supply stores.

A number of companies make very good templates. A favorite kind is the precision metal model with a nonskid back. It comes in all the common shapes and sizes: triangles, hexagons, squares, and so on. A number of plastic varieties are also marketed, and some books are printed with a section of cardboard templates that can be cut out and used right from the book. Templates also come in the shapes of favorite quilting designs, and there are some lovely antique ones in wood and metal, greatly prized by collectors.

See also: Patterns, Quilting, Stencils

THEME QUILTS

A quilt may be designed with a theme for many reasons, but the main one is to qualify it to be entered in a contest. Of course, the Bicentennial produced many theme quilts, by individuals and by groups.

Some contests are for quilts celebrating

LEFT: **Window templates by Ardco in many basic pieced-quilt shapes. These are metal with a nonskid back and a built-in seam allowance**

RIGHT: **To celebrate the Coast Guard's 200th Anniversary, a quilt contest with a theme of ships and sea was held. The third place winner in the small wall-quilt category is Our Ocean Star by Nancy Parmelee of California. 36 x 36″**

the first manned space flight, a 200th anniversary of statehood, or other grand themes. These contests can also be for individual blocks on a theme — the winning ones being joined into a full quilt for display.

Individuals occasionally make theme quilts for their families, colleges, or other very personal reasons. Women have always celebrated such things as their gardens and their states with the designs in their quilts. In a sense these are thematic.

See also: Bicentennial quilts, Block contests, Contests

THIMBLES

The constant pressure of needle against finger necessary for making a fine quilting stitch requires the use of a thimble, just as tailors and seamstresses have always worn thimbles. Most people wear this metal or plastic guard on the third finger of the hand that holds the needle. Some quilters wear a thimble or other guard on a finger of the opposite hand also. Several new designs of thimbles and other finger-guards have appeared in recent years to meet the demands of quilters.

See also: Quilting

THREAD

Quilters have many choices to make when they start to create a quilt — pattern and design, fabric, batting, and even thread. In other centuries and other societies the choice was often not as wide as it is now. In times of real poverty women even quilted with thread retrieved from old garments or the seams on feed and grain sacks.

Cotton was not always so common a fiber in Europe as we think of it today. Prior to 1800 many quilts would have been stitched in silk, wool, or linen. An early name in the manufacture of cotton sewing thread was the still-familiar Clark of Coats and Clark. This company was also a leader in the field when the advent of sewing machines made it necessary to refine and strengthen thread. The letters O.N.T., known to generations from the midnineteenth century into the latter half of the twentieth, stood for Our New Thread. It is sometimes helpful in dating a quilt to examine the thread.

Several companies have manufactured

OPPOSITE PAGE: **The grand prize winner of the Coast Guard's 200th Anniversary contest is The Lights Along the Shore by Elsie Vredenburg of Michigan. 76 x 95″**

LEFT: **Thimbles used by quilters vary greatly according to personal preference: on the left, two simple plastic thimbles, one adjustable in size; the leather thimble in the background is a favorite, as is the metal one with a rim; the three in front, made of silver and decorated, are serviceable**

RIGHT: **Clark's Thread Co. supplied spool chests to stores that sold their "New Thread" in the nineteenth century. Collection of the author**

A throw in Victorian crazy quilt style, made by Anna Houston Brackett of Denmark, Iowa, ca. 1880. It is shown here in the parlor of Terrace Hill, Des Moines, the Iowa governor's mansion

threads specifically for quilting. For many years an unmercerized cotton thread, white or black, was made in a variety of sizes or weights — the larger the number, the finer the thread, so that baby clothes would have been sewn in size 100 and work clothes in size 30, for example. Some women making utility quilts used these heavy threads.

The first practical synthetic fiber was rayon, appearing in about 1920 and extremely popular in the Great Depression because of its fine look at a low price. It did not appear in sewing thread at that time, but Coats and Clark has recently developed a high-quality rayon thread for machine- or hand-sewing. It remains to be seen whether it will make its way into quilting. After trying all the synthetic and combination threads of the last decades, many quilters have returned to high-quality, all-cotton threads for piecing, appliqué, and quilting. *See also: Fabrics, Fibers, Quilting*

THROWS

The Victorian era was a time of elegance, comfort, and, we may say, clutter. Every dresser or table had a scarf, embroidered and edged, and every sofa had an afghan or two or a throw, frequently in the form of a small silk or silk and velvet quilt. Webster's Dictionary defines a throw as a "light scarf" or "cover," but it is doubtful whether these quilt confections were ever used to cover a reclining body. It may be that so many fine examples of Victorian throws survive because they were never used in any way that might damage them. Today's less formal "nap quilts," often made for people in nursing homes, are the direct but more useful descendants of the Victorian throws.

See also: Victorian crazy quilts

TIED QUILTS

Having a warm bed covering in earlier times was a necessity in unheated homes, so it was very important that these covers be made quickly. It would have been impossible for every covering to be meticulously quilted in intricate designs. The alternative was to tie the three layers together with small lengths of yarn every few inches. These ties then became a sort of decoration on the surface of the quilt or comfort. If a sturdier filler were used, such as wool (which clings together better than cotton), or even an old blanket, the cover would last longer. Such quilts were usually pieced of simple squares or strips, rather than in complicated designs.

Another type of quilt that was frequently tied was the Victorian crazy quilt. Silk thread or ribbon made the ties, and sometimes there were decorations of buttons or beads fastened to them. As these quilts rarely had batting and were rather stiff, there would be no way to quilt them in designs.

See also: Comforters, Haps, Victorian crazy quilts

TIE-DYEING

In recent years tie-dyeing has been once again very popular for T-shirts, play clothes, and background fabric for modern quilts. The process is another ancient one from the East, adapted to American usage. It is also called "tie-and-dye," which perhaps better describes the actual process. Small portions of the fabric are tied off with waxed thread and then the pieces are dipped in dye. The result is a series of interesting, slightly runny, circular bands of color that bleed into one another on a dark background.

The Japanese carried this process to its ultimate decorative possibility in designs called *shibori*. The dots created by tieing are so minute that they look like tiny bubbles on the fabric. The most elaborate of these, done in the seventeenth century, may be seen in museums and special exhibitions.

See also: Dyes

TOBACCO PREMIUMS

Both the small silk ribbons that came in some cigarette packs in the early twentieth century and the silk strips that were used to wrap packets of cigars are sometimes called tobacco premiums.

See also: Cigar band silks, Cigarette premiums

TOPS

A quilt has three layers: top, batting, and backing. The top is the decorated fabric, whether pieced, appliqué, embroidered, or stenciled, or it is the right side of a whole-cloth quilt. In a well-made whole-cloth or two-sided quilt it is hard to tell which is the top. For purposes of putting the layers in the frame, however, one side is always the uppermost, or "best."

In antique shops and secondhand stores it is possible to find some quite wonderful tops that were completed but never backed, batted, or quilted. If the fabric is still strong, it may be sensible to finish them, but it does not usually enhance their value to the collector. Buying tops is a good way to acquire quilts with an antique look for country-style decorating without paying too high a price.
See also: Backings, Batting

Trapunto, sometimes mistakenly called corded quilting, ca. 1790. This quilt came down through the Simons/Armstrong family of Charleston, South Carolina, and New York. The fabric is very fine, perhaps linen, and the channels are filled with soft yarn. 90 x 105″. Courtesy of the Charleston Museum. (Detail)

TRAPUNTO

Certain terms are bandied about in relation to quilting without being very clearly defined. Somehow trapunto and stuffed work have come to mean the same thing. Trapunto originated in Italy, as early as the sixteenth century and possibly before. In both trapunto and stuffed work the design is raised on the surface of the fabric by means of some type of filler inserted between layers. True trapunto seems to have been worked in smaller and narrower areas, appearing almost to be corded. Stuffed work, as often seen on Early American quilts, especially the great wool ones, had large, more rounded areas, stuffed from the back with batting or wadding pushed between the threads of the weave or through a slit made in the backing.

For trapunto, a lightweight backing is stitched to the surface fabric with two parallel rows of running stitch. A large, blunt needle is then used to bring soft, resilient yarn through the weave of the fabric to raise the area between the rows of stitching. Sometimes this is referred to as "corded" quilting.

Trapunto has been very popular on clothing in the recent quilting revival. Marge Murphy is the best-known designer and teacher in this field. She uses delicate silk and silklike fabrics to produce blouses, skirts, and even elaborately worked wedding gowns, as well as whole quilts.
See also: Marseilles spreads, Stuffed work

TREE MOTIFS

Before the age of instant communication, design was most often based on the familiar objects of everyday experience. In quilt design, this meant that stars and puzzles and birds were common themes. Flowers and trees have been featured in both appliqué and pieced design since quilts were first decorated — and long before that in many other types of needlework and embroidery.

Pieced block design was particularly American, and several Tree of Life and Pine Tree motifs appeared soon after the more English chintz appliqué Tree of Life designs fell from fashion — probably between 1840 and 1860. Toward the end of the century, pattern companies picked up existing ideas and created yet more. The Live Oak Tree and Forbidden Fruit Tree were variations on tree themes, all pieced in triangles and diamonds. The Temperance Tree, which is very similar to other tree designs was, like the

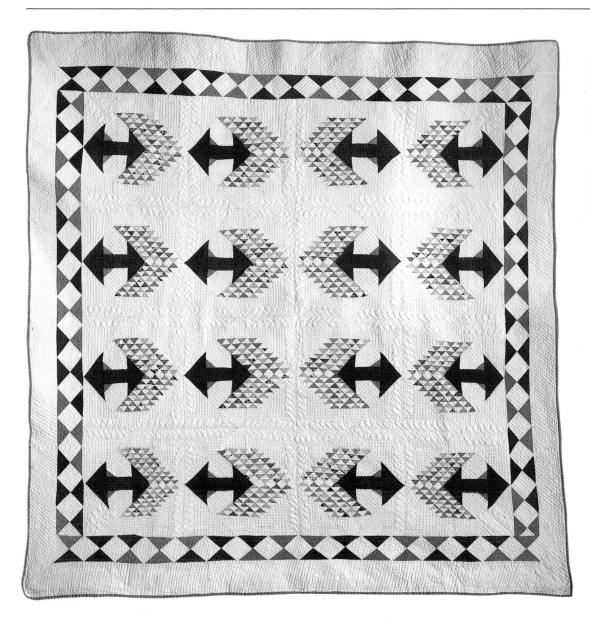

LEFT: **Pieced Pine Tree designs have been popular since the midnineteenth century. This one is signed Ursel Layman, New York State, 1865-70. 72 x 76". Courtesy of Roslyn House, Quilts, Country Antiques**

BELOW: **Detail of a Trail of the Lonesome Pine quilt, probably from a Nancy Cabot pattern. Collection of Susan Parrish, Antiques**

Drunkard's Path, symbolic of the temperance movement of the late nineteenth and early twentieth centuries.

In the twentieth century, several companies published patterns called Trail of the Lonesome Pine, a theme made popular in a song of the same era. Another simple pattern of the same time is usually called Tall Pine Tree. It has been popular with contemporary art quilters because of its bold outline and many possible variations.

See also: Tree of Life

RIGHT: **This chintz appliqué quilt from the Hammond family of Virginia is thought to have been made by the three consecutive wives of the oft-widowed Captain Thomas Hammond. Mary Tapscott Hammond probably started it in 1793, a year after her marriage. She died shortly thereafter, and Mildred Washington Hammond may have worked on it between 1797 and 1804. Between 1807 and 1835 Ann Collins Hammond must have finished it, as the roller print used in the border stems from that time period. The block-printed Tree of Life pieces in the center date from the late eighteenth century. 96 x 94″. Collection of the Kenmore Association, Fredericksburg, Virginia**

OPPOSITE PAGE: **Equilateral triangles, dark and light, usually scrap, form a traditional design known as Thousand Pyramids. The prints in this one are from the late nineteenth century. Collection of the Blue Hill Historical Society in Maine. (Detail)**

TREE OF LIFE

Quilts made just before and after 1800 with a large appliqué tree in the center were called Tree of Life quilts. The designs were cut out from Indian palampores or bedcovers and were often enhanced and elaborated with additional birds, animals, and other chintz cutouts.

The hill of earth on which the tree was always placed was known as the *"terra firma* mound" and represented an idealized ver-

sion of the world abounding in flora and fauna. The same motif was used in Jacobean embroidery or crewel work. Though these designs came originally from India and Persia, they were Anglicized as the demand for such goods increased in Great Britain and the United States.

As pieced quilt patterns became more elaborate and more numerous in the nineteenth century, a Tree of Life made up of many triangles appeared and is still current.

The Tree of Life continues to be a popular motif for quilters, sometimes appearing as a center for medallion quilts and sometimes used as a family tree.

See also: Broderie perse, Palampores, Tree motifs

TRIANGLES

Two types of triangles are used in quilt design — the equilateral and the right-angle. The old favorite Thousand Pyramid pattern is made up of rows of equilateral triangles fitting neatly together. For greater impact, the design calls for a row of dark fabric triangles with the points up and then a row in light fabric, points down. The right-angle triangle is made quite simply from a square cut across diagonally, enabling it to be used in many patterns made up of squares, like the nine-patch.

See also: Geometry, Nine-patch designs, Octagons

FOLLOWING PAGE: **Each 60°
diamond in the ever-popu-
lar Tumbling Blocks has
been cut into nine little diamonds and pieced in scrap,
each piece of different fabric, making it a charm quilt.
Called A Trip to Mother's
Attic, it was made by Carol
Brown of Minnesota.
82 x 104″**

TUMBLING BLOCKS

A design that has existed a lot longer than quilts have is now called Tumbling Blocks. It is a one-patch design that uses only 60° diamonds. The trick is to make them of light, medium, and dark fabrics, so that they look like the top and two sides of a block, in accurate perspective. Each block forms a complete hexagon and can be used in more elaborate patterns with other hexagonal pieces.
See also: Geometry, Hexagons, One-patch designs

UTILITY QUILTS

Some quilts are made as works of art, displayed on beds only for special occasions, never used as covers for warmth. Others, the utility quilts, can be made of anything from men's worn-out suits to cotton feed sacks. They are often thick, filled for warmth with lumpy homegrown cotton or wool, an old blanket, or another quilt too worn to use. One interesting version of the utility quilt is a "soogan," made in the southwestern United States for cowboys and herdsmen, as part of their bedrolls.
See also: Comforters, Depression quilts, Feed sacks, Haps, Wool

VELVET

It is fairly unusual to find an all-velvet quilt. The thickness of the fabric and its somewhat slippery texture make it difficult to seam, especially in the small pieces required for a quilt. In Victorian crazy quilts the pieces were often laid flat on the foundation, with the next piece, often of a thin silk, turned under over the raw edges. This method avoided the worst problems of

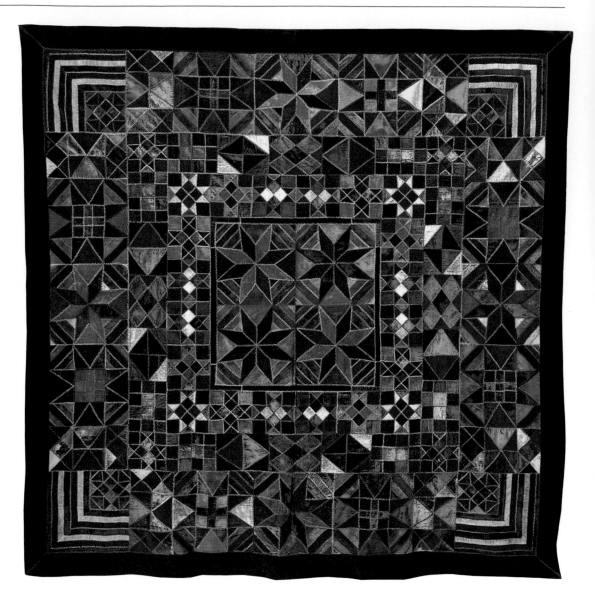

seaming, pressing, and having seams meet at the corners. In the few examples of all-velvet quilts, elaborate embroidery is often used over the seams, probably to make them lie flat and to control the entire pattern of the piecing. These demanding quilts were made by very skilled seamstresses.

See also: Foundation piecing, Victorian crazy quilts

VICTORIAN CRAZY QUILTS

Though we tend to think of the crazy quilt as a product of poverty-inspired thrift, that is not the case with the elaborate Victorian crazy quilts that burst upon the scene in 1880. With their silks and velvets and complex embroidery, they were a part of the Art Needlework Movement espoused by such people as Louis Comfort Tiffany and Candace Wheeler. Fine fabrics, infinite numbers of embroidery stitches, and no confining pattern made this type of quilt much more closely related to needlework than to quilting.

Such quilts — usually throws for the sofa — were made and used as decoration well into the twentieth century. They fell from

favor by 1920 and for the next fifty years were not highly prized by quilt collectors. Fortunately, many museums received them as parts of other collections, and Victorian crazy quilts have been preserved and are now shown and prized on their own merits.

Silk often deteriorates more rapidly than other textiles, so the preservation of Victorian crazy quilts is difficult. They have been saved to some degree by the fact that they are usually foundation-pieced, with little pull or stress on the silks.

See also: Foundation piecing, Silk, Velvet

There is so much good in the worst of us,
And so much bad in the best of us,
That it scarcely behooves any of us
To talk adout (sic) the rest of us.

Detail from a Victorian crazy quilt made by Edna Force Davis of Fairfax County, Virginia. Many sentiments and moral sayings were embroidered on quilts at this time, and especially on crazy quilts. Courtesy of The Smithsonian Institution, Washington, D.C. Gift of Miss Hazel Davis

ABOVE: Late Bloomer, a pieced and appliqué wall hanging by Anna Holland of Waterford, Virginia, 1988, is made in an Early American style and of antique fabrics

RIGHT: The professional term for washing a quilt is "wet cleaning." It is done on a special table so that the water runs gently through the fabric. Courtesy of the Textile Conservation Center, South Salem, New York and Patsy Orlofsky

W WALL QUILTS

Now that quilts have been acknowledged as an art form, they are often hung on walls for decoration. A full bed-size quilt is difficult to deal with in most spaces — it follows that a quilt made solely for decoration can be any size desired. Wall quilts have burgeoned in this century along with art quilts and miniatures, the three being more or less indistinguishable categories. For purposes of judged shows, the groups may be aligned in any way that makes the judging easiest and most fair.

Wall quilts are especially suitable for pictorial or scenic themes and such personal formats as family trees. For those artists who are skilled with the sewing machine, this is an original and appealing field.
See also: Art quilts, Genealogical quilts, Miniature quilts, Pictorial quilts, Scenic motifs

WAR QUILTS

Just as there are quilts on the themes of peace and other causes, war has been enough a part of women's lives for them to express their feelings about it in their quilts. The Red Cross quilts of World War I were often made as fund-raisers, though possibly just a burst of patriotic enthusiasm inspired them in some cases.

As far back as the Civil War, quilts recorded the sentiments of the times, incorporating flags and other patriotic symbols. Though World War II came during a period when quilting was beginning to fade in popularity, there were quilts decorated with "V for Victory" and portraits of important wartime figures. As the war came to an end and Americans became aware of the desperate conditions in Europe, some quilts were made to be sent overseas in a reversion to their original purpose of keeping people warm.
See also: Cause quilts, Patriotic quilts, Peace quilts, Political quilts, Red Cross quilts

WASHING

The wet cleaning of antique quilts is a controversial subject. There is even considerable disagreement about how to wash a quilt made as an everyday bedcover. Some problems can be avoided when a new quilt is planned. If the fabric is prewashed to deter-

The cartoon figures of sailors and the date, 1944, pinpoint this quilt by Carrie Lake of Goodland, Kansas, as a tribute to the young men of the U.S. Navy in World War II. Each figure bears the name, and sometimes the rank, of some "hometown boy." Some are marked "Prisoner" and some "Killed in Action." 78 x 90". Collection of America Hurrah, New York City

mine color fastness and to deter further shrinkage the washability of a new quilt is to a large degree ensured.

There are mild soaps and detergents suitable for washing quilts. The choices are the same as for any other fine fabrics, except that there is a liquid now on the market created specifically for quilts, Ensure, made by Mountain Mist, the batting manufacturer.

If a new quilt fits into a washing machine and the controls allow the cycles to be adjusted forward so as to soak with very little agitation, and spin only enough to get the heaviest amount of water out, machine washing can be safe for most utility quilts.

Washing by hand in a tub is a two-person job, as a wet quilt is incredibly heavy and cumbersome. Because there is really no way

Kim Masopust created an evening coat titled God Save the Queen for the Fairfield Fashion Show. She used traditional Cathedral Window and appliqué techniques, presenting portraits of several queens of Henry VIII on the front and the king himself on the back

to get the water out thoroughly, several rinses are necessary to remove soap film. The old-fashioned method of drying by spreading the quilt flat on a sheet in a shady place out-of-doors, though perhaps the best, is not practical for everyone. The washing machine and a short cool run in the dryer are in general more practical.

See also: Conservation

WASTE CANVAS

Cross-stitch or counted-thread embroidery are easily worked on even-weave fabrics, because the symmetry of the stitches can be gauged by the number of threads in the background. If cross-stitch is to be worked on the finely woven fabric of a quilt for purposes of applying names and dates, a loose, open-weave canvas can be basted over the fabric and the embroidery worked through the canvas. When it is completed, the waste canvas can be pulled apart, one thread at a time, and thus removed so that the embroidery stands alone on the quilt fabric. Labels for the backs of quilts are often made to look like samplers on waste canvas over the muslin.
See also: Labels, Stitches

WEARABLE ART

Quilting has always been used on clothing and has had a place in fashion, but wearable art — sometimes known as art-to-wear — is a fairly new departure. Quilt artists like Virginia Avery, Yvonne Porcella, and Jean Ray Laury are known for wearing their own designs, elaborately decorated with appliqué, piecing, and quilting. This clothing is a far cry from the strip-pieced and quilted vests and other simple garments worn today by many quilters and craftswomen — it is truly original and elaborate art.

In 1979 Fairfield Processing Corporation saw the trend and mounted their first Fairfield Fashion Show of wearable art at the Houston Quilt Festival and Market. Donna Wilder has been in charge of planning and producing what has become an extravaganza of beautifully decorated high fashion — about fifty pieces each year. In their tenth anniversary year Fairfield produced a book

There are a number of Wedding Ring patterns but the most familiar one is the Double Wedding Ring. This one, in startling red and scrap, is African-American, made in Atlanta, Georgia, in the Depression years. 86 x 73″. Collection of Dr. Robert Bishop

of pictures and commentary about the shows through the years.

In some cases the garments are based on commercial patterns but the decoration is all individual and exuberantly original. Many techniques are used — other needle-work, painting, and stenciling, as well as quilting techniques of all kinds. Artists frequently work all year to produce these wearable works of art, which may be seen at several shows throughout the year.

See also: Clothing, Companies, Fashion

WEDDING RING DESIGNS

Quilts were always made for brides or by young women preparing to marry, but the

Typical Welsh quilting designs on a whole-cloth quilt, made in 1933 by the Porth Quilting Group, under the Rural Industries Bureau Scheme. The quilt was presented to the Welsh Folk Museum, St. Fagans, Wales

Wedding Ring designs are relatively new in quilting. There is an ongoing controversy about the exact origins of the design and especially whether it was ever made in its present form or forms much before 1900. Patterns for the Double Wedding Ring were available in newspapers and from pattern companies early in the twentieth century and grew in popularity through the Depression. It has been called "the most often-made pieced pattern in the entire repertoire of American quiltmakers," and its popularity in those lean years might in part be attributed to the fact that these striking designs could be made from scraps. New versions appeared during this period: the Golden Wedding Ring, Bridal Bouquet, and several others.

In 1989 *The Romance of Double Wedding Ring Quilts*, by Robert Bishop, appeared, complete with pages and pages of colorful examples and patterns for several varieties. Research for the book had not, however, unearthed the origin of the pattern or exact information about its first appearance.
See also: Brides' quilts, Marriage quilts

WELSH QUILTS

Quilts were mentioned in sixteenth-century Welsh records. The oldest-known surviving ones are from the eighteenth century and are in the Welsh Folk Museum at Saint Fagans. Two types predominate in any reference to or collection of Welsh quilts — whole-cloth and medallion. The medallion quilts, like those from England, depend on the selection of fabrics rather than elaborate piecing designs. The whole-cloth quilts, like those from the North of England, are of superb design and workmanship. Fine wool batting is used in most Welsh quilts.

Itinerant quilters were familiar in the villages and farms of Wales through the eighteenth and into the nineteenth centuries. It is said that many of these women, working full days and often by candlelight way into the night, could produce a beautifully quilted bed quilt in two weeks. They were poorly paid, but they received their room and board at each house, as did seamstresses during the same period in America.

Welsh quilting is, like that from the North of England, so expertly patterned and worked that most of the quilts can be used on either side. The reverse of the medallion quilts is often as attractive in design and craft as the whole-cloth quilts.

In the twentieth century, efforts have been made to revive Welsh quilting as a cottage industry. Mavis Fitzrandolph, historian and author of *Traditional Quilting*, was sent to Wales during the Great Depression by the Rural Industries Bureau to help in the reorganization of quilting for profit. There were enough quilters to start this project. Classes were arranged so that younger women could be taught and the tradition of excellent quilting kept alive. Teachers like Jesse Edwards of Porth saw that characteristic Welsh designs were passed on and the quality maintained. The quilts were sold in London and other large centers, and occasional exhibitions were mounted. Some of the quilts from the RIB Scheme are now in the Welsh Folk Art Museum.

See also: English quilts, Irish quilts, Medallion quilts, Whole-cloth quilts

WHITNEY MUSEUM SHOW

There have been many great quilt shows and exhibitions throughout the last century or so, but probably none with the impact made by "Abstract Design in American Quilts" at the Whitney Museum in New York in 1971. Jonathan Holstein and Gail van der Hoof collected graphic American quilts and presented them in this exhibition to what seems to have been a waiting world.

Suddenly, people who had never contemplated a quilt as anything more than a bedcover were talking about the show as they would have about a new artist who had burst upon the scene. All kinds of people, many with little prior needlecraft, started making Bicentennial quilts. Groups formed, and more shows were organized. "Abstract Design" at the Whitney was a watershed in the development of the American quilt.

See also: Amish quilts, Bicentennial quilts, Collectors

WHOLE-CLOTH QUILTS

A quilt that is neither pieced nor appliqué, but is decorated solely with quilting is called a whole-cloth quilt. It can be all white or of any color. The wool quilts of eighteenth century America are whole-cloth as are the early silk, linen, or cotton quilts of Europe. Certain areas, such as Wales and the North of England, are noted for their handsome whole-cloth quilts.

See also: All-white quilts, English quilts, Linsey-woolsey, Quilting, Welsh quilts

WOOL

Probably the most universal fiber for cloth is wool, whether from sheep, goats, or llamas. It is easy to spin, warm, and can be dyed in lovely colors. Quilts have not only been made of wool but have also been filled with wool batting for several hundred years. Many wool quilts of the eighteenth century can be found in museums, but there are fewer examples from the early nineteenth century on.

In the late nineteenth century, wool reappeared in Victorian crazy quilts and Log

Miniature version of a whole-cloth or all-white quilt, made by Sharon Crosswhite of Missouri in 1989. 15 x 16". Collection of the author

FOLLOWING PAGE: Appliqué and embroidered quilt by Pocahontas Virginia Gay of Fluvanna County, Virginia, ca. 1900. Wool was a much-used fabric in Victorian quilts. This one combines crazy-quilt blocks with pictorial ones, including the Southern heroes Andrew Jackson, Jefferson Davis, and Robert E. Lee on the right, and "His Master's Voice" second from left, third row from the bottom. 68 x 66". Courtesy of The Smithsonian Institution, Washington, D.C. Gift of Mr. and Mrs. Edward Garvey

Cabin quilts. Today's art quilters experiment with many fabrics, but wool is not used widely, perhaps because of its current prohibitive cost. Wool batting, however, is seeing something of a resurgence thanks to its warmth and excellent needling qualities.

See also: Batting, Fibers, Linsey-woolsey, Log Cabin, Victorian crazy quilts, Whole-cloth quilts

LEFT: Wool was often used in Amish quilts, like this Star one from Lancaster, Pennsylvania, ca. 1890. The wool colors remain bright and pure a hundred years later. 81 x 75″. Collection of the Museum of American Folk Art, New York. Gift of Phyllis Haders

BELOW: One of the many WPA quilting projects was the making of bedcovers for needy families. This group was being mounted for display at the 1937 Minnesota State Fair. Minnesota Historical Society, St. Paul

WPA

Many agencies in Washington during the Roosevelt years were devoted to helping people deal with the Depression. One of the best known, the Works Project Administration, served the artists and artisans of the country in a number of ways. In the case of quilters, they set about to produce a quilt index as part of the WPA's *Index of American Design.* In several locations, quilts were listed and meticulously realistic paintings made of blocks or of entire quilts. Much of the information garnered is available to quilt researchers and historians at the National Gallery of Art Library in Washington, D.C.

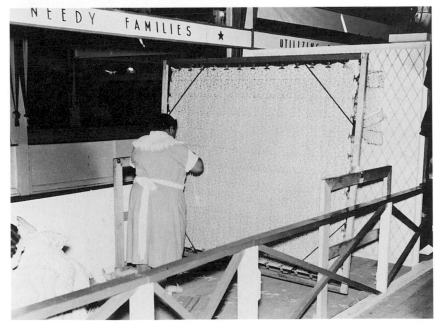

One WPA project under the division called Index of American Design preserved traditional quilt patterns. A set of thirty from a Pennsylvania Museum Extension Project, South Langhorne Division, has recently been reprinted and some patterns are shown here. Plates, 19 x 13″

In WPA workshops quilters were also encouraged to design and make quilts, a few of which survive in various collections. Eleanor Roosevelt took especial interest in our national arts and crafts, including quilting. *See also: Depression quilts*

WRITERS

The twentieth century has witnessed an interest in recording the making of quilts and the lives of the makers. In the years before World War II there were researchers and writers who preserved the lore of nineteenth-century quilts. Many of them, like Marguerite Ickis (*The Standard Book of Quilt-Making and Collecting*), Ruth Finley (*Old Patchwork Quilts and the Women Who Made Them*), and Carrie Hall (*The Romance of the Patchwork Quilt*), were either quilters or collectors themselves. In England, Averil

Colby and Mavis Fitzrandolph recorded the history of quilts of the British Isles.

The quilting revival sparked by the American Bicentennial has produced such a massive outpouring of books that it would be hard to list them all. They can be divided into several categories, with some of the most prolific and best-known authors mentioned:

Quilt history: Among writers on this subject are Thomas K. Woodard with Blanche Greenstein, *Twentieth Century Quilts, 1900–1950*, Barbara Brackman, *Clues in the Calico*, Sandi Fox, *Small Endearments*, Jeannette Lasansky, *Pieced by Mother*, and researchers like Virginia Gunn who write mainly for magazines and research publications.

Books of instruction and patterns: As more people become interested in quilts, their needs seem to change. The team of Gwen Marston and Joe Cunningham writes attractive books of information and instructions, complete with patterns, such as *American Beauties: Rose and Tulip Quilts*. Carla Hassel wrote two manuals for the absolute beginner and the novice quilter, so complete that they can easily take the place of classes. One of them is *You Can Be a Super Quilter*. Jinny Beyer's *Quilter's Album of Blocks and Borders* and Roberta Horton's *Calico and Beyond* tell how to plan quilts, using traditional patterns and exciting color and fabric combinations. Georgia Bonesteel's books are based on her lap-quilting methods and come with full-size patterns and color pictures.

The list of current authors of quilt books is startlingly long and appears to be growing. A look at your local library's card catalogue index will surprise and reward you. *See also: Designers, Lap quilting, Quiltmakers, Researchers and historians, Teachers*

Yo-Yo

A Yo-Yo spread, while not actually a quilt, always appears in information about quilts. It consists of only one layer — there is neither batting nor backing. The process is simple and the result can be quite attractive.

Small circles of fabric (about the size of a yo-yo) have a gathering thread run around the edge of each circle. This is then pulled tight so that the piece is double, one side smooth and one side showing the gathered edge. They are then sewed together by hand for about a half-inch along each edge. The joining leaves a small opening between each group of four circles. The Yo-Yos are sometimes arranged in a design and sometimes, as with a scrap quilt, in random patterns of color. Such novelties as the Yo-Yo and the similar Cathedral Windows designs reached the height of their popularity in the period from 1920 to 1930.

See also: Cathedral Windows

INDEX